POWER PRAYERS

POWER PRAYERS
Warfare that Works

Sheila Zilinsky & Carla Butaud

© 2016 by Sheila Zilinsky and Carla Butaud. All rights reserved.

No part of this publication may be reproduced, stored in a retrieval system, or transmitted in any way by any means—electronic, mechanical, photocopy, recording, or otherwise—without the prior permission of the copyright holder, except as provided by USA copyright law.

Unless otherwise noted, all Scriptures are taken from the Holy Bible, King James Version, © 1979, 1980, 1982 by Thomas Nelson, Inc., Pub-lishers. Used by permission.

Scripture references marked NKJV are taken from the New King James Version, © 1979, 1980, 1982 by Thomas Nelson, Inc., Publishers. Used by permission.

Scripture quotations marked NIV are taken from the Holy Bible, New International Version®, NIV®. Copyright © 1973, 1978, 1984 by Biblica, Inc.™ Used by permission of Zondervan. All rights reserved worldwide.

Scripture references marked NLT are taken from the Holy Bible, New Living Translation, copyright © 1996, 2004 by Tyndale Charitable Trust. Used by permission of Tyndale House Publishers, Wheaton, Illinois 60189. All rights reserved.

ISBN: 978-1543140637

TABLE OF CONTENTS

Introduction, vii
1. Morning Warfare Prayer, 13
2. Prayer for Our Nation, 16
3. Prayer Against Evil Systems in America, 19
4. Prayer for Your Child/Teen, 21
5. Prayer for School Children, 23
6. Prayer for a Child Being Bullied, 25
7. Prayer for Prodigals, 26
8. Prayer Concerning Arrested Development, 28
9. Prayer for Healing, 31
10. Prayer Concerning Weather, 33
11. Prayer Over Meals, 35
12. Prayer Concerning Air, Water and Food Supply, 36
13. Prayer Concerning Weapon Systems, 39
14. Prayer for Travel—Part 1, 41
    Prayer for Travel—Part 2, 43
    Prayer for Travel—Part 3, 44
15. Bedtime Prayer, 46

16. Prayer Concerning Marriage-Blocking Spirits, 47
17. Prayer Concerning Mental Torment, 50
18. Prayer Concerning Conflict, 54
19. Prayer Concerning Poverty and Lack—Part 1, 58
    Prayer for Ministry Finances—Part 2, 62
20. Prayer Concerning Cleansing Possessions, 63
21. Prayer Concerning Blood Covenants and Oaths, 65
22. Prayer Before and After Surgery, 67
23. Prayer Against Bondage, 68
24. Prayer Against Satanic Attack, 70
25. Prayer Concerning Soul-ties and Sexual Sin, 72
26. Prayer Concerning Forgiveness, 76
27. Prayer Against Generational Curses, 78
28. Prayer Against the Antichrist Spirit, 80
29. Prayer Against the Spirit of Death, Including Abortion, 83
30. Prayer Against Abortion and the Shedding of Innocent Blood, 87
31. Prayer Against the Curse of the Firstborn, 90
32. Prayer Against the Spirit of the Bride of Satan, 92
33. Prayer Against the Curse of the Bastard, 95
34. Prayer Against the Curse of Tamar, 100
35. Prayer Against the Curse of Jezebel and Ahab, 104
36. Prayer Against the Spirits of Incubus and Succubus, 108
37. Prayer Against the Spirit of Leviathan, 111
38. Prayer Against the Spirit of Kundalini, 113
39. Binding and Loosing, 118
40. Do I Have To Know The Name Of A Spirit To Bind It Or Cast It Out?, 120

What Must I Do to Be Saved?, 122

Glossary of Terms, 125

INTRODUCTION

The power of prayer is astonishing! The power of the Living God is activated by prayer, especially when combined with regular fasting, which are vital together. Prayer is one of our biggest weapons against the enemy and the demonic hosts of hell. That is why it is so important that we as believers learn how to pray effectively. Many times warfare prayer is treated as a last resort—when it should be our first resort! The Word says in James 5:16, "The effectual fervent prayer of a righteous man availeth much."

There has never been a time in history when warfare prayer was so urgently needed. As the end days fast approach, never before have we witnessed such a callous disregard for God and prayer. It is treated as a side note and a last resort, all while gross teaching, seducing spirits, and false doctrines abound. Ubiquitous debauchery and abhorrent sin are the order of the day as the church has become weak and anaemic, becoming nothing more than glorified social clubs with very little power.

The greatest tragedy facing modern believers today is disregarding, ignoring, and denying the power of the demonic realm. Supernatural powers of the forces of darkness require supernaturally empowered believers. The only way to stand against the wiles of the enemy is to be armed with the Word of God and to know how to use tactical warfare. Satan has been operating undetected and unhindered by the saints of God for too long. It's time for the church to begin to operate in the power and authority that Jesus shed His blood for, that we might do as He did . . . to destroy the works of the enemy! (See 1 John 3:8.)

We have superior weaponry, equipment, and power but unfortunately most believers are woefully ignorant and living far beneath their birthright and their inheritance from God. As we crash headlong into the beginnings of the terrible tides of wickedness sweeping the world, religious clichés and formulas will not work when it comes to our enemy. In the days ahead, the ability to lay hold of the power of God may easily determine the difference between life and death. Those unaware of or who deny the power of the demonic realm shall be helpless in the face of the coming all-out assault from the spirit world.

It is vitally important for us to know the difference between prayer and warfare. Prayer is addressing God, warfare is addressing the enemy. *You cannot leave out the*

part where you are addressing the enemy. In this book we combine the two. In Exodus 14:16 God told Moses to use the rod of authority that He had given him! And it's time we take our rod of authority and take back ground. It is time we acted like the soldiers of Jesus Christ that we are instead of weak and anaemic Christians. A soldier doesn't win by hiding in offense mode. No war was ever fought and won like that. It is time we starting warring against the real enemy. We are not fighting flesh and blood (see Eph. 6).

It is time that we as believers stopped living in frustration, hopelessness, defeat, and bondage. It is an affront to what Jesus did on the cross. Our fight is a spiritual one. We cannot see into the spiritual realm but it is every bit as real—if not more real—than what you see in front of your face. It is time to use the authority that God has given you through His Son Jesus Christ.

Here are just a few examples from the Word of God:

Psalm 60:12 "Through God we shall do valiantly: for he it is that shall tread down our enemies."

Matthew 21:22 "Whatsoever ye shall ask in prayer, believing, ye shall receive."

Mark 11:24 "Therefore I say unto you, What things soever ye desire, when ye pray, believe that ye receive them, and ye shall have them."

Psalm 107:28 "Then they cry unto the Lord in their trouble, and he bringeth them out of their distresses."

Mark 9:29 "And he said unto them, This kind can come forth by nothing, but by prayer and fasting."

Acts 9:40 "But Peter put them all forth, and kneeled down, and prayed; and turning him to the body said, Tabitha, arise. And she opened her eyes: and when she saw Peter, she sat up."

James 5:15-16 "And the prayer of faith shall save the sick, and the Lord shall raise him up; and if he have committed sins, they shall be forgiven him.
Confess your faults one to another, and pray one for another, that ye may be healed. The effectual fervent prayer of a righteous man availeth much."

Ephesians 6:18 "Praying always with all prayer and supplication in the Spirit, and watching thereunto with all perseverance and supplication for all saints."

Philippians 4:6-7 "Be careful for nothing; but in everything by prayer and supplication with thanksgiving let your requests be made known unto God. And the peace of God, which passeth all understanding, shall keep your hearts and minds through Christ Jesus."

Luke 10:19 "Behold, I give unto you power to tread on serpents and scorpions, and over all the power of the enemy: and nothing shall by any means hurt you."

Matthew 17:20 "And Jesus said unto them, Because of your unbelief: for verily I say unto you, If ye have faith as a grain of mustard seed, ye shall say unto this mountain, Remove hence to yonder place; and it shall remove; and nothing shall be impossible unto you."

There are also five key components to powerful and effective prayers. Here are those keys:

1. Being a born again, saved believer through receiving the Lord Jesus Christ as your Saviour (see Rom. 10:9-10). **STOP HERE!** The contents of this book are pointless without this step, so proceed to page 122—What Must I Do to be Saved?
2. Repentance, renunciation, and turning from your sin and wrongdoing (this is ongoing). (See Acts 26:18; 2 Cor. 6:17.)
3. Obedience to the full gospel of Jesus Christ (see Luke 11:13, 24:49) as a committed disciple of Jesus Christ on the earth (see Acts 1:8).
4. Surrender to God, seeking endowment of the power of the Holy Spirit (see Acts 1:4-15; 2:38-39; 5:32, Rom. 8:1-2, 8-10, 13-16; Gal. 5:16-26; Col. 3:17), as in the book of Acts—receiving water baptism

and being baptized in the Holy Spirit as evidenced by speaking in tongues. Know your position and authority in Jesus Christ.
5. Learn to pray in faith in accordance with the Word of God (see Eph. 2:6, Acts 3:16; 4:12; John 14:12-15; 16:23-26; Col. 3:17; John 15:7-16; 13:35, James 1:5-8; Heb. 11:6).

We get many, many prayer and deliverance requests from believers all over the world who require help with a variety of afflictions. We began to see a huge need for the development of this book. We dedicate this book to you, all those that have requested it. These prayers were developed after being beaten up and robbed by the devil. We spent years allowing the enemy to wreak havoc and cause destruction in our lives and our families' lives because we were unaware that there was something we could do about it. These prayers were literally birthed when hell came to our front door. We only wish we could have had these prayers many years ago. These prayers are powerful and these prayers work! Believe it! It is our sincere hope that you and your family will be immensely blessed by this book.

May God richly bless you as you step out in His power!

We love you,
Carla and Sheila

1
MORNING WARFARE PRAYER

Note: We have found it very helpful to address the enemy even before we start our day. When you make phone calls or have personal conversations that you don't want the enemy to hear, say out loud, "Lord, I cover this conversation with the blood of Jesus, and I bind every little bird that would carry my words. In Jesus' name." (See Eccl. 10:20.)

Father, in the name of Jesus, I thank You for giving me power over all the power of the enemy (see Luke 10:19).

I exercise that power now and I bind and break the power of the spirit of the witch, the wizard, the warlock, and the witch doctor. In the name of Jesus, I bind and break the power of every spirit from the kingdom of darkness working against me and [names of person(s) or ministries, etc.].

I bind every evil spirit, even from those in the kingdom of light, charismatic witchcraft, etc. and in the name of

Jesus, I break the power of every word or spoken curse being spoken against me and [names of person(s) or ministries, etc.].

I send out the warring angels (see Heb. 1:14) to scramble the plans and the assignments that the enemy has for me this day.

I sever the silver cord of every spirit that is astral-projecting[1] to watch me, eavesdrop, gather information, trip me up, block, or hinder the works of God! In the name of Jesus, I bind every spirit not of the Holy Spirit.

Satan, I bind you, rebuke you, and render you powerless over my life and [name of church, ministries, family members, etc.].

I assign mighty angels to stand shoulder-to-shoulder around [names of person(s) or ministries, etc.] to guard and protect so that no evil can penetrate.

Father, deliver us from evil (see Luke 11:4). I ask that you would expose any terroristic acts and unholy activity before it has time to take root.

Give me keen discernment and wisdom that I might be as wise as a serpent, but harmless as a dove (see Matt. 10:16), and I thank You now for turning every curse that would come against me or mine into a blessing for our good and Your glory. (See Num. 24:1-9; Deut. 23:5.)

---

[1] Astral projection or travel denotes the demonic practice of leaving the physical body.

I cover myself, [names of persons, ministries, etc.] with the precious blood of Jesus Christ this day.
In Jesus' name,
Amen and amen.

2

PRAYER FOR OUR NATION

Father, thank You for giving us power over all the power of the enemy. I exercise that power now, and in the name of Jesus Christ, I assign the mighty angels that you have given to assist me (see Heb. 1:14) to discover and expose every plot of violence, death, and destruction before it is put into action. I assign mighty angels to stand shoulder-to-shoulder around [town, city, country] with their flaming swords drawn so that no one with destructive agendas can enter in.

Father, I pray for Your will for this nation and if possible I ask for restoration of our nation. You say this is a people robbed and spoiled, all of them snared in holes and hidden in prison houses. They are for a prey and none delivers; for a spoil and none says restore (see Isa. 42:22). Lord, I ask You to cause it to be reported in the third heaven this day that we say unto You, "Lord, deliver and restore" because I know restoration is only by Your power (see Judg. 11:13-24). I speak restoration over all areas bound.

In the name of Jesus Christ, I bind the Strongman[2] over this nation and the spirits of political and spiritual blindness. I bind the Strongman over each individual state, commonwealth, territory, possession, and all land occupied by the United States of America [enter in your country].

I come against violence and destruction in our nation. I bind the Strongman over terrorist groups and religious violence and break their power. I bind and break the power of the spirit of the prince of the power of the air that works in the children of disobedience (see Eph. 2:2). I bind the spirit of murder, suicide, death, and destruction. We bind and break the power of the spirit of Ishmael: jealousy, hatred, murder, retaliation, and I forbid them to operate.

I speak confusion to the enemy's camp. I bind and break their communication lines and I send out warring angels to scramble and cancel the enemy's plans and cause the enemy to turn on itself and leave none standing as happened in the Old Testament.

I cover myself with the blood of Jesus Christ and call on mighty angels to stand around us, me and my family, and Your saints all over this world shoulder to shoulder, that *no evil penetrate.*

---

[2] See **Bind the Strongman** in Glossary page 125

Father, I ask Your spirit of truth to be loosed upon the people. Loose godly sorrow that leads to repentance, salvation, and redemption onto the lost sheep of our nation, in Jesus' name.

Lord, You have revealed Your nature to us in the names You have given Yourself. In Your name, Elohim, You are the Covenant Keeper and the Eternal and Unchanging God. I am Abraham's Spiritual Seed (see Gal. 3:16, 29) and all the promises of God are Yea and Amen in Jesus Christ.

In Jesus' name,
Amen and amen!

3

PRAYER AGAINST EVIL SYSTEMS IN AMERICA

Note: This prayer can be tailored to other countries and their respective organizations.

In the name of Jesus I bind the Strongman over and the evil spirits of the: Illuminati, Trilateral Commission, one world government, Council of Foreign Relations, World Council of Churches, socialism, humanism, Marxism, all Muslim organizations, one world currency, Federal Reserve System, inflation/collapse of economy, Federal Reserve, United Nations, the President, Vice President, State Departments, Congress, Supreme Court and judicial system, all governmental advisors—official and unofficial, all forms of military, IRS, all regulatory departments of the government.

I loose into these systems the Spirit of the Lord (Isa. 11:2). I loose love, power, peace, truth, a strong economy, inventiveness, understanding, loyalty to God, riches, honor, glory, strength, blessing, wisdom, and knowledge. I loose into America great favor from the Lord.

In Jesus' name,
Amen and amen!

PRAYER FOR YOUR CHILD/TEEN

Note: It's best to cast spirits out of your child while he or she is asleep. Simply go to your child's bedroom door; they do *not* have to be actively involved. You don't have to pray so loud that it wakes the child up since demons have supernatural hearing. You also don't have to know what to call the spirit.

Declare this prayer out loud: "You spirit that is causing [name of child] to be [fill in the blank with whatever the undesired manifestation is, for example, rebellious/shy/awkward, etc.], I bind you, break your power, and command you to *go*! In the mighty name of Jesus Christ.

"I loose upon [name of child] the [desired manifestation, for example, if you're dealing with rebellion you would loose obedience, if you're dealing with fear you would loose peace, etc.]. I loose upon the child the fruit of the Spirit," and if the child is saved you can say, "I activate the mind of Jesus Christ."

In Jesus' name,
Amen and amen!

5

PRAYER FOR SCHOOL CHILDREN

Note: Have your child pray with you where possible out loud, taking turns if there's more than one child.

Father, in the name of Jesus, I thank You for this day. I thank You for [child's name].

I assign mighty angels to stand around [child's name, name of school, teachers, and each student of your town, city, country] shoulder to shoulder that no evil can penetrate. I bind all spirits that would try to teach my child unGodly things.

I speak a supernatural ability to my child's mind to retain what he/she learns today and supernatural recall when taking tests.

I loose God's supernatural favour on [child's name], as well as favour with his classmates and teachers, etc.

I bind every spirit of rebellion that would cause [child's name] and others to misbehave and get into trouble.

I loose upon [child's name], a spirit of peace, obedience, and respect for himself/herself, teachers, and others.

And I thank You, Lord Jesus, for a great, happy, and blessed day.

In Jesus's name,
Amen and amen!

6

PRAYER FOR A CHILD BEING BULLIED

Note: If your child is being bullied at school, pray with them before they go to school.

Declare this prayer out loud,

Father, I send the mighty angels to accompany [name of your child] to school and stand guard. Father God, I ask You to open the eyes[3] of the bully that he would see the angelic protection around [child's name] and stay away from [child's name].

I bind the spirit of the mean-man[4] in the bully and forbid it to operate.

In Jesus' name,

Amen and amen."

---

[3] In 2 Kings 6:17 — "And Elisha prayed, and said, Lord, I pray thee, open his eyes, that he may see. And the Lord opened the eyes of the young man; and he saw: and, behold, the mountain was full of horses and chariots of fire round about Elisha."

[4] Spirit of the Mean Man—See Glossary of Terms page 126

PRAYER FOR PRODIGALS

Father, in the name of Jesus, I lift up every prodigal son and every prodigal daughter of Your saints all over the world. (If your child is a prodigal, you can also include his or her name).

I call on mighty warring angels to go and war in the heavenlies over each of their lives for the battle that is going on for their souls.

I bind the Strongman over each one and break his power over their lives and command him to *loose them* in the mighty name of Jesus. I break off of them bondage to drugs, alcohol, addictions, self-destructive behaviors, oppression, depression, lawlessness, homosexuality, pornography, perversion, sexual sins, and rebellion, in Jesus' name.

I call on Michael the archangel (see Dan. 12:1), who stands for the children of Thy people to assist in the battle.

I bind and break the power of the antichrist spirit, religious spirits, and the spirit of the prince of the power of the air that works in the children of disobedience.

I loose the love of God, the spirit of repentance, salvation, and deliverance upon each prodigal. I ask, Father, in the name of Jesus, that You would send Your Holy Spirit and ministering angels to begin to minister to them in dreams and visions, and woo them back into the kingdom of heaven and the family of God. And in the name of Jesus, I speak a supernatural maturity to every spiritual seed that has been planted in them and call them to take root and bear fruit.

Mighty godly women, *come forth*, in Jesus' name! Mighty godly men, *come forth*, in Jesus' name!

I thank You, Father, that everything Satan has brought into their lives for bad, You will turn around for their *good* . . . and Your *glory*!

I remind you, Satan, that my children have been trained up in the way they should go, and they received the seed of the Word of God which remains *forever*, and at some point, they will serve God with all their hearts, and they will be a force to be *reckoned with*! Now Satan, in the name of Jesus Christ of Nazareth, I command you to *loose them—and let them go*.

In Jesus' name,
Amen and amen!

PRAYER CONCERNING ARRESTED DEVELOPMENT

This is a prayer about "arrested development." This means that a person's mental, physical, or spiritual growth can be stunted, slowed, or weakened while being formed in the womb, or any time trauma is experienced along life's way. Arrested means: to bring to a stop, to slow, to make inactive, seize, capture, to take or keep in custody by authority of law; with development it means: growth that has stagnated and which slows down or stops.

Essentially, arrested development is when growth has stopped in some area. This can be caused by trauma in the womb or trauma in childhood or later years. Examples include Muscular Dystrophy (muscles arrested), Down Syndrome (Mongoloid); retardation (brain cells arrested); Epstein-Barr virus; bodily functions and day-to-day skills; bed-wetting; visual and audio problems; stunted motor skills; stunted growth, learning disabilities; slow reader;

Dyslexia; mental block; fears and insecurities; social problems, confusion; spatial, motor, and other perceptual deficits; memory problems; impulsivity; short attention span; OCD, ADD, childishness, doesn't want to leave security by growing up, tantrums and fits, childish self-will, immaturity, laziness, always wanting their way, irresponsible, inability to put away childish things, rejection; fear of rejection; mental abuse by parents; over dependence on others; anger; frustration; outcast, etc. When praying over someone else, have the person sit in a chair, stand behind them, and place your hands on the sides of their head.

Father, in the name of Jesus Christ, I bind and break the power of generationally inherited arrested development and command it to go. Spirit of arrested development in [name of person]'s brain that is causing problems, I bind and break your power, and I command you to go now in the name of Jesus. I bind and break all spirits of trauma and fear.

All arrested development that occurred while [name of person] was being formed in the womb, I break your power and *command you to go*, in the name of Jesus Christ. I speak a *supernatural maturity* to the mind and emotions of the healthy 0-12 month-old baby [boy or girl]. I speak healing to their brain in Jesus' name.

I bind and break the power of arrested development that took place in [name of person] between the ages of one and five and in the name of Jesus, I speak a *supernatural maturity* to the mind and emotions of the healthy one-year-old, two-year-old, three-year-old, four-year-old, five-year-old (call the years one by one). I speak healing to their brain in Jesus' name.

I bind and break the power of arrested development that took place in [name of person] between the ages of six and ten and, in the name of Jesus, I speak a *supernatural maturity* to the mind and emotions of the healthy six-year-old, seven-year-old, eight-year-old, nine-year-old, ten-year-old (call the years one by one. Once you get to age 10, use increments of 10, i.e., 10-20, continue on following the exact prayers that we've provided above).

In Jesus' name,
Amen and amen!

PRAYER FOR HEALING

Note: Ideally it is best to go to the elders of your church as that is the order God set up (James 5:14) and wives should go to their husband, who is the head and the priest of the home, and put a demand on his position as priest of the home. (See Eph. 5:23). Using anointing oil (simple olive oil will do) and praying for the person is ideal, but because there is no distance in the spirit you can pray this over any sick person or you can tailor this prayer to apply it to yourself as well if you have any type of illness or affliction.

Father, I thank You for Your Son, Jesus Christ, who gave His life on the cross. Lord, I thank You that You shed every drop of Your blood in order that the world might be saved, healed, and delivered!

I thank *You* that *You* suffered this [name of infirmity] when *You hung on the cross* so [name of person] wouldn't have to suffer it.

I bind and break the power of the curse of death that came to all of us through Adam. I bind and break the power of the spirit of infirmity, the ruler spirit over all infirmities, and I command it to leave [name of person's] body now in Jesus' name.

I bind and break the power of [name of infirmity or affliction]. I speak death to it from the root out and command it to leave his body now in the name of Jesus Christ.

I apply the shed and resurrected blood of Jesus Christ to [name of person's] entire body and say, "Body, be healed in the name of Jesus! [Name the body part], be healed in [name of the person], in Jesus Christ's name!"

Last, but not least, the *grace that is sufficient*, the grace Jesus poured out on Calvary when He declared, "*It is finished!*" That's the grace I apply to [person's name]'s body, in Jesus' name.

Father, we receive it by faith and thank You for it right now.

In Jesus' name,
Amen and amen!

PRAYER CONCERNING WEATHER

Note: This can be used in your town, city, or region, depending on where you live, for all types of weather, including earthquakes, storms, tornadoes, hurricanes, wildfires, flash floods, mudslides, etc.

Father, I thank You for giving me dominion over the fowl of the air, over the fish of the sea, over the cattle and over every creeping thing, and over all the earth! (See Gen. 1:26.)

I exercise dominion now over this approaching weather. I bind all damaging winds, damaging hail, damaging lightning, flooding, the formation of tornadoes, and all damaging weather. We bind death and desruction, in the name of Jesus.

I assign mighty angels to stand around my city, my property, my possessions, and my family, shoulder to shoulder that no evil can penetrate.

Jesus said, "Peace, be still" to the storm—and it obeyed!
I also say, "Peace, be still" to the [applicable weather].
In Jesus' name,
Amen and amen!

11

PRAYER OVER MEALS

Note: It is very important to always pray over *all* our food, even snacks. When eating in a restaurant it is not necessary to pray some loud, long-winded prayer, but softly is recommended. Whether at home or eating in public, it is very important to always pray over your food. If you are uncomfortable praying aloud when eating with a group, a quiet or even a silent prayer is fine.

Heavenly Father, we thank You for this food. Please bless, purify, and cleanse it so that we can be fit temples for the Holy Spirit to reside in. We break any curses on it and speak a neutralization to anything harmful in this food. We eat it with thanksgiving and we now cover this food with the blood of Jesus.

In Jesus' name,
Amen and amen!

12

PRAYER CONCERNING OUR AIR, WATER AND FOOD SUPPLY

Note: This includes things like genetically modified objects, plots in chemtrails, geoengineering/HAARP, etc.

Father, in the name of Jesus Christ, I thank You for giving us *dominion* (Gen. 1:26). "And God said, 'Let us make man in our image, after our likeness: and let them have dominion over the fish of the sea, and over the fowl of the air, and over the cattle, and over all the earth, and over every creeping thing that creepeth upon the earth.'"

We stand on your Word in Psalm 112:1, 6-10:

> Praise ye the Lord. Blessed is the man that feareth the Lord, that delighteth greatly in his commandments. Surely he shall not be moved for ever: the righteous shall be in everlasting remembrance. He shall not be afraid of evil tidings: his heart is fixed, trusting in the Lord. His heart is established, he shall not be afraid, until he see

his desire upon his enemies. He hath dispersed, he hath
given to the poor; his righteousness endureth for ever;
his horn shall be exalted with honour. The wicked shall
see it, and be grieved; he shall gnash with his teeth, and
melt away: the desire of the wicked shall perish.

Father God, in the name of Jesus, I speak neutralization to the chemicals being poured out in the atmosphere through chemicals in the air, water, and food (including chemtrails, geoengineering/HAARP, etc.)[5]

I speak neutralization to any harmful chemicals being put in the air, water, or food supply, i.e., genetically modified objects (GMOs). I thank You for Your Word that says, "For every creature of God is good, and nothing to be refused, if it be received with thanksgiving, for it is sanctified by the word of God and prayer" (1 Tim. 4:4-5).

---

[5] Chemtrails are long-lasting trails left in the sky by high-flying aircraft consisting of chemical or biological agents deliberately sprayed for purposes undisclosed to the general public. Geoengineering is the deliberate large-scale intervention in the Earth's natural systems to counteract climate change. HAARP is the High Frequency Active Auroral Research Program, an ionospheric research program jointly funded by the U.S. Air Force, the U.S. Navy, the University of Alaska, and the Defense Advanced Research Projects Agency (DARPA).

I cover myself today with a protective shield of the blood of Jesus Christ that no evil touch me and my family. May we not eat or drink any deadly thing.

In Jesus name,
Amen and amen!

13

PRAYER CONCERNING WEAPON SYSTEMS

Note: For the purpose of this prayer, our definition of a weapon system includes: inflicting death or injury on, or damaging or destroying a person (or the biological life, bodily health, mental health, or physical and economic well-being of a person) through the use of land-based, sea-based, or air-based systems using radiation, pulsed microwaves, electromagnetic, psychotronic, sonic, laser, or other energies directed at individual persons or populations for the purpose of mood management, mind-control, or manipulation of human behavior with the use of any and all weapons whether subliminal, sound, or visual, visible or invisible, devices using frequencies, manipulation, etc.

Father, in the name of Jesus Christ, I thank You for giving us power over all the power of the enemy and even the tools the enemy uses for manipulation and control as in weapon systems coming against us in this toxic soup we are being bathed in every day.

Father God, Your Word says "No weapon that is formed against thee shall prosper; and every tongue that shall rise against thee in judgment thou shalt condemn" (Isa. 54:17) and in the name of Jesus, I bind and break the power of every weapon and weapon system being used against me/us, including land-sea- and air-based systems. I bind and break *all* frequencies and energies being used against me and my family for any evil purpose and speak a neutralization and reversal of every tactic of the enemy to manage, control, or manipulate me whether subliminal, sound, or visual, visible or invisible, in Jesus' name. Even things I am not aware of, I break the power of all of it in the name of Jesus.

I speak confusion to the enemy's camp, and I send out the warring angels to scramble every weapon system the enemy has in Jesus' name.

I cover myself and my family with a protective hedge and impenetrable shield and I cover us with the blood of Jesus and I call on mighty angels to guard and protect us no matter where we are.

In Jesus' name,
Amen and amen!

PRAYER FOR TRAVEL— PART 1

Father, in the name of Jesus, I thank You that You have given me dominion. I exercise that dominion now over the fowl of the air and over everything that creeps on the earth, and I command them to stay out of my roadway.

I speak supernatural, mechanical, and physical preservation over this automobile. I speak supernatural gas mileage and supernatural travel time. Lord, if possible, I ask that You would translate me to my destination.

I bind every rock and loose article on the road to the road, and every spirit that causes accidents, in Jesus' name.

I bind and break the power of curses placed on the roadways and bind every bloodthirsty spirit that hovers over the highways. And I bind all spirits of harassment from city policemen and highway patrolmen, and I command you to *be occupied* when I pass through your city! In the name of Jesus.

While I am away, I appoint mighty angels to stand guard around my property, shoulder to shoulder, that no evil penetrate, and I thank You for a safe trip . . . to and from.

In Jesus' name,
Amen and amen!

PART 2—HOTEL AND ACCOMMODATIONS

Upon entering hotel room/place of accommodation, declare out loud:

"Father, in the name of Jesus, I bind every unclean spirit in this room, break their power, and command them to *get out* . . . and every familiar spirit to *go*! I cover everything in this room with the blood of Jesus to be cleansed and sanctified while I am here. I invite angels to not only encamp around the external space (i.e., outside the room) but I invite them to inhabit this internal area (i.e., inside the room) to guard and protect me and all my belongings for the duration of my stay, and I thank You, Father.

In Jesus' name,
Amen and amen!

PART 3—AIRLINE TRAVEL

Father, in the name of Jesus, I thank You that You have given me dominion over the weather (see Gen. 1:26). I speak to the weather for [dates of travel/trip – to and from], and I call for clear, calm weather in the atmosphere. I bind the spirit of the prince of the power of the air. I bind all turbulence, delays, and any other upheavals that can occur with air travel.

I commit every detail of this trip to You. I ask You to orchestrate who will pilot the plane . . . who the flight attendants will be . . . even who will be flying with me.

I employ mighty angels to escort my plane to and from my destination safely. I employ angels to accompany my luggage, so that it makes it to my destination with me.

I bind spirits of accidents and incidents and all spirits of infirmity while I am away.

I stand mighty angels around my home, family, and possessions shoulder to shoulder while I am gone.

I pray for Your favor to be upon me on this trip. I send out the angels to be posted all the way to assist me in whatever way I might need them, and I thank You ahead of time, Lord, for my way being pleasant, prosperous, and successful in every way. And last, but not least—Satan, I bind you, rebuke you, and render you powerless over this trip.

In Jesus' name,
Amen and amen!

15

BEDTIME PRAYER

Father, in the name of Jesus, I bind every spirit that would come to torment me in my sleep—even my dreams. I employ mighty angels to stand around me while I sleep, shoulder to shoulder that *no evil* penetrate! I say to my mind, *Peace, be still.*

In Jesus' name,
Amen and amen!

PRAYER AGAINST MARRIAGE-BLOCKING SPIRITS

Note: First make sure you have dealt with and removed the soul-ties (see Soul-Ties Prayer page 72).

Proverbs 18:21-22 "Death and life are in the power of the tongue: and they that love it shall eat the fruit thereof. Whoso findeth a wife findeth a good thing, and obtaineth favour of the Lord."

Father, in Jesus' name I renounce all sin in all areas and I close any door I may have opened to Satan through contact with the occult, New Age, Ouija board, astrology, fortune telling, hypnosis, ESP, etc.

(Confess anything that you can think of that you may have been involved in that you need to renounce and repent from. Ask God to help reveal things to your mind and when you finish renouncing them, notify the devil): "I am closing the door against all these things I know about and all the things I don't know about. I renounce you and all your demons and I am closing every door I may have opened."

Father, by the power of the blood of the Lamb and the grace of God, I break every stronghold of opposition and generational hindrances that would hinder me from receiving a godly mate.

In Jesus' name, I take authority over curses and generational reaping and sowing the enemy uses to hinder me from being married. In Jesus' name I break and destroy spirits of separation and divorce in my family line. I bind and break spirits of isolation and loneliness trying to hold me in a state of not finding a godly mate.

I break all curses spoken by past mates, friends, family members, or even that I have spoken over myself, in Jesus' name. I break all verbal curses, negative speech, ungodly slander, rumours, and discord being sown against me from past partners/spouses, all character assaults and curses from anyone speaking negatively against me. In the name of Jesus, I declare that no weapon formed against me shall prosper.

Father, if I have knowingly or unknowingly done something by word, action, or deed that the enemy is using to hinder, block, or obstruct me from finding and marrying a godly mate, then I repent, ask You to forgive me, and I nail it to the cross where it is blotted out by the blood of Jesus—no longer having legal authority or power over my life. In Jesus' name I bind all marriage-breaking spirits, hindering, blocking, and obstructing spirits prohibiting me from finding and marrying a godly mate. Go now in Jesus' name.

I bind and break the power of the spirits of the broken heart that caused me not to trust people, nor want to deal with a partner because of past hurt. All spirits that came in from betrayal, abandonment, fear, rejection, and hurt, go now in Jesus' name.

I take authority over the power of demonic spirits that would cause me to be pursued by the wrong type of man/woman. All the familiar spirits that cause me to be attracted to the wrong mate, go in the name of Jesus.

I thank You, Lord, that I am a favored woman/man and a blessing from the Lord. The godly man/woman who finds me obtains favor of the Lord!

In Jesus' name,
Amen and amen!

PRAYER CONCERNING MENTAL TORMENT

Note: You can also pray this for someone else who is being attacked by inserting their name in place of yourself.

Statistics now estimate that one in every 5 people (that is conservative) struggle with some type of mental illness/mental disorder[6]. Sadly, it is ubiquitous in today's church and what is even sadder is that it is not being addressed. There is a tendency to avoid discussion of mental illness to avoid the stigma or label that seems to inevitably attach to the victims. Let us dispose of that idea, for we are dealing with demons and the symptoms they create and foster. Mental illness is not a mere sickness or disease, but a combination of demonic entities. Their program is to drive you

---

[6] http://www.macleans.ca/authors/julia-belluz/mental-illness-does-it-really-affect-one-in-five/

insane and they usually work at this gradually. Tormenting like a cancer, they exact the maximum in suffering until the human breaks down. The battlefield in which the demons work is your mind. The sins of the fathers is one of the main reasons for mental illness as it passes from generation to generation through the blood line. Mental affliction can take on labels such as Panic Attack, Bipolar, Manic Depressive Disorder, Personality Disorder, Schizophrenia, and the list goes on. Suicide multiplies at an alarming rate in response to the unbearable stresses and strains of everyday life without natural affection. Depression has become an outright epidemic. Many soldiers return home with Post-traumatic stress disorder (PTSD) which is triggered by witnessing terrifying events, causing severe trauma. This term mental illness/mental disorder is actual rooted in torment, double mindedness, confusion, and fear. These spirts of infirmity and torment can even cause a chemical imbalance causing the afflicted person to seek medication to help them "feel" normal again. This results in medicating the symptoms, but not getting to the root of the problem. When people seek pharmaceuticals they are only compounding the problem. The modern term "pharmacology" (where we get pharmacist, pharmacy, etc.) emerged from "Pharmakeia"[7] which means

---

[7] Strong's Concordance-pharmakeia: the use of medicine, drugs or spells
Original Word: φαρμακεία, ας, ἡ
Part of Speech: Noun, Feminine

sorcery or witchcraft. One variation means a *"spell-giving potion"* by a witch or magician. Drugs were most commonly used in pagan worship to hallucinate and to try to get in touch with evil spirits. (Matthew 17:14-17, Acts 10:38, Galatians 5:20, 2 Thessalonians 2:2, Isaiah 47:9; Exodus 7:11, Exodus 7:22; Exodus 8:18, Revelation 9:21, Revelation 18:23, Revelation 21:8).

Prayer: Father, I repent for and renounce all whoredom, idolatry, sin and rebellion including witchcraft and sorcery, even from my ancestors that may have caused curses or openings for mental infirmities, affliction, torment and bondage to operate. In the name of Jesus Christ, I bind all generationally-inherited mental illnesses. I bind the strongman of all mental illnesses and infirmities and break your power and command you to get out of my mind now, in the name of Jesus Christ. I bind and break all spirits of Bipolar, confusion, deception, delusion, depression, distrust, doubt, double-mindedness, forgetfulness, frustration, hallucinations, insanity, indecision, indifference, incoherence, lunacy, madness, mania, mind-binding, paranoia, Personality Disorder,

---

Transliteration: pharmakeia
Phonetic Spelling: (far-mak-i'-ah)
Short Definition: magic, sorcery, enchantment
Definition: magic, sorcery, enchantment.
5331 pharmakeía (from pharmakeuō, "administer drugs") – drug-related sorcery, like the practice of magical-arts, etc. (A. T. Robertson).

PTSD, persecution, procrastination, rebellion, retardation, senility, Schizophrenia, suspicion, trauma, vexation and command you to get out now in Jesus name. All tormenting spirits I command you to leave. Any and all spirits that came in through any form of drug use, including alcohol, tobacco, marijuana, etc. All Pharmakeia, witchcraft and sorcery spirits I bind and break your power and command you to go now in the name of Jesus. I bind every word spoken, every curse cast over me including labelling me as "mentally ill" or "crazy." I speak neutralization to the unnatural chemicals that have been released in my brain, and command them to be balanced the way God designed. I speak PEACE to my mind—I say PEACE BE STILL to my spiritual, mental, emotional and physical body. I give leave to every familiar spirit of mental torment and mental illness and I say, *Mind Be Healed!* In Jesus' mighty name. Father you have not given me a spirit of fear; but of power, and of love, and of a sound mind. I now loose that sound mind to myself.

In Jesus' Name,
Amen and amen.

PRAYER CONCERNING CONFLICT

Father, in the name of Jesus, I take authority over all the spirits having to do with conflict. I bind and break the spirit of offense and being over-sensitive and touchy. I come against strife, combat, contention, being contrary, meanness, mean spiritedness, go in the name of Jesus.

All evil spirits, the flip-flop spirit—being spiritual one minute and acting like the devil the next—I bind that flip-flop spirit in the name of Jesus and command it to go.

Spirits of opposition, division, upheaval, taking things the wrong way, spirit of offense, go in the name of Jesus. Wrath, evil speaking, gossip, spreading gossip, corrupt communication, I bind you and break your power and command you to *go*, in Jesus' name.

Hypocrisy and the spirit of hypocrites, I bind you and break your power and command you to go in the name of Jesus.

I tear off the mask, wearing a mask, putting on a happy face, skirting the issue, walking around pretending. I bind the spirits of pretender, false presentations, and lying spirits.

Telling a lie, talebearing, being a troublemaker or a busybody, spirits of perversion, I bind you and break your power and command you to go, in Jesus' name.

Bearing false witness, spreading of lies, sowing discord, slander, hearsay, accuser of the brethren, character assassination, which is spiritual murder, the critical spirit who's always looking to criticize people, I bind you and break your power in Jesus' name.

I come against accusations, finger-pointing, bullying spirits. Go in Jesus' name.

Imaginations (sometimes you're just imagining it, a lie believed as fact,) all spirits of presumption (presuming things, having no proof to back up what you think or say,) I bind you in Jesus' name.

Hard-heartedness, stony heart, unforgiveness, bitterness, anger, resentment, retaliation, and revenge, *go*, in the name of Jesus.

Fear Spirits, fear of being honest, fear of man, fear of confrontation, all Fear Spirits and cowardice, I bind you and command you to *go*, in Jesus' name.

Hiding from the issues, skirting the issues, denial, pride, stubbornness, rebellion, and disobedience, I bind you and break your power in Jesus' name.

Counterfeit peacekeeper spirit—that perverse spirit of just doing whatever needs to be done to bring the peace—I bind that counterfeit peacekeeper spirit in Jesus' name. I loose the genuine original peacemaker spirit in its place (blessed are the peacemakers), being honest, loving, speaking the truth in love, and being reconciled, in Jesus' name.

I bind grudges and holding grudges, in the name of Jesus. (People have this in their families—sisters who have not spoken to each other in thirty years, aunts who haven't spoken to someone after one little something happened.) I come against division—division in families, division in churches, division in marriages, division in friendships. *All* division *go*, in the name of Jesus.

Religious spirits and haughtiness, I bind you and break your power, in Jesus' name.

I bind hurt, injury, grief and sorrow caused by conflict and command these spirits out in Jesus' name.

Control is actually witchcraft. Control using emotional blackmail and manipulation, control with anger, control with silence, attitudes, and behaviors, control with money, control with fear, and control with pouting, etc. (whatever they are controlling with,) I bind that spirit of control and break it *now* and command it to *go* in Jesus' name. I give leave to all familiar spirits of control, *go*, in the name of Jesus. I give leave to every spirit not of the Holy Spirit. All familiar spirits go now in Jesus' name.

We thank You, Lord, that we're going to look at conflict differently from now on. We're going to look at it from Your Word's perspective. I bless [fill in the blank or use your name here] and I loose upon them gentleness and meekness; grace and truth, and love, honesty, openness, the courage to go and be reconciled, courage to apologize if it's necessary, transparency—not hiding the truth, the ability to forgive and the ability to reconcile, reconciliation, justice, unity, peace, understanding, speaking the truth in love, sincerity, boldness, virtue, and gratitude of heart, in Jesus' name.

Lord, I ask You to take out the stony hearts and circumcise their hearts and pour out Your love so that they can respond in love, instead of responding out of hurt. I ask You to bless them and ask that You give them peace in their minds, hearts, souls, and spirits, in the name of Jesus. We loose the mind of Christ and restore them back to you now.

In Jesus' name,
Amen and amen!

19

PRAYER CONCERNING POVERTY AND LACK—PART 1

Note: We find that owing money (slave to the lender) is one of the biggest blocks to God's blessings. It is imperative that if you have outstanding debts with anyone (this can include people, businesses, collection agencies, etc.—if you cannot recall, then ask the Holy Spirit to reveal to you anyone you owe money to). Even if many years have passed, make your best possible effort to clear the debt and pay back what you owe. If you cannot pay the entire amount, then make an agreed payment arrangement. Make a genuine effort to pay back all monies, even ones you may have legitimately forgotten about. Ask the person to forgive you for your error in not paying it. It doesn't matter how the person responds (anger, not willing to forgive, bitterness, etc.). It is about your godly action of integrity—not their response. Finally, ask God to forgive you where you have erred and not paid your debts; and then forgive yourself. Also it is vitally important to sow into where you are being spiritually fed and helped through tithes and offerings.

Father God, Your resources are vast and unlimited. You own the cattle on a thousand hills. Everything belongs to You and we are rich because Jesus paid the price when He reconciled us back to You. I will not put my trust in my job, my salary, or my bank account but I will put my trust in You. I repent and ask You to forgive me for not believing properly and appropriating Your Word properly in the area of finances, giving and receiving. Father God, I repent where I have failed You and ask forgiveness where I have missed it or opened a door to poverty and lack.

I bind and break deception and idolatry, New Age, witchcraft, disobedience and general sins that opened a door for the poverty and lack spirits to operate in my life. Every generational curse having to do with lack, poverty, and slavery on both sides of my family all the way back to Adam and Eve, I break your power in Jesus' name. I bind all poverty demons, mindset of poverty, mindset of lack, mindset of slavery, which is idolatry and witchcraft. I come against hindering spirits, blocking spirits, obstructing spirits and I command you to go in Jesus' name. I give leave to the following spirits—debt, slave to the borrower, bankruptcy, stubbornness, headstrong, obstinate, self-spirit, spirits of idolatry, independent, impulsiveness, rashness, careless, hasty, intellectualism, lack, poverty, deprivation, insufficiency, unyielding, and every spirit that goes contrary to God, every spirit that perverted God's Word in the area of blessings, giving and receiving, lawlessness, criminal minded, disobedience, nonconformity, corruption, withdrawal, suspicion, mistrust, jealousy, envy, pessimism, cynicism, doubt, disbelief, discontentment. All fears, go now in Jesus' name. I give leave to all the familiar spirits in the name of Jesus. I bind, rebuke, and break the assignments of the devourer (see Mal. 3:11) now in Jesus' name.

The Scripture says the wealth of the sinner is laid up for the just (see Prov. 13:22) and I now call for a release of the wealth of the wicked to be brought into the hands of the righteous for the kingdom of God. I now command every demon that has funneled my resources, devoured my prosperity, and robbed me of my blessings to *go now* in Jesus' name. Satan, I bind you, rebuke you and render you powerless over my income, finances and prosperity.

I now loose the harvesting angels to go and gather up and bring every single thing that was stolen and robbed from me to be returned into my storehouse. I am calling in the double portion[8] now in Jesus' name. Father, I ask now

---

[8] Isaiah 61:7 "For your shame ye shall have double; and for confusion they shall rejoice in their portion: therefore in their land they shall possess the double: everlasting joy shall be unto them." Job 42:10 "And the Lord turned the captivity of Job, when he prayed for his friends: also the Lord gave Job twice as much as he had before." So it could be said that Job received a "double portion."

for the floodgates of heaven to be poured out on me and my family.

I loose Your spirit of favour in the area of my income, finances, and prosperity in all areas that concern me in the name of Jesus, and I give You thanks.

In Jesus' name,
Amen and amen!

PART 2—PRAYER FOR MINISTRY FINANCES

The following is specific for finance concerning those in ministry: Father in Jesus Name I ask you to send Your Holy Spirit and Your ministering angels to lay it on the hearts of all those who have been blessed by the gift of God in me—to sow into the ministry that You have entrusted to me, in order to advance Your kingdom. I pray for Your supernatural favor and expansion on this ministry and give You thanks.

In Jesus' name,
Amen and amen!

20

PRAYER FOR CLEANSING POSSESSIONS

Note: It is a good idea to anoint your home with oil. This can be done every few months. It is also a good idea to walk around your property and bless it. Also, ask God to reveal anything in your possession that is not glorifying to Him and remove the object(s). Every single thing that you buy is manufactured, and we don't know the people or materials pertaining to *all the things you've purchased and brought into your home*. Here are just a few examples: food and grocery items, make-up, hygiene products, clothes, books, souvenirs from trips, religious items, movies, especially items bought in second-hand stores/garage sales, jewelry, artwork, etc.

Deuteronomy 7:26 says, "Neither shalt thou bring an abomination into thine house, lest thou be a cursed thing like it: but thou shalt utterly detest it, and thou shalt utterly abhor it; for it is a cursed thing."

Father, in the name of Jesus, I bind and break the power of all witchcraft, hexes, vexes, and curses that have been placed on all items in my possession. I give leave to all familiar spirits and curses that have attached themselves to all items in my possession. I break evil soul-ties with whoever manufactured these items. I break all evil soul-ties with the person or persons who gave me any items with ill will.

I bind and break the curses and evil soul-ties on every item that I have in my possession in the name of Jesus, and I bless them to be a blessing.

I cover my home, my property, and all my possessions with the blood of Jesus Christ.

In Jesus' name I pray,
Amen and amen!

PRAYER CONCERNING BLOOD COVENANTS AND OATHS

The circumcision was a blood covenant between God and His people. So theoretically, whenever there is a breaking of skin on your body, a blood covenant is formed. Even if you are unaware of it, Satan will use anything he can to get a foothold. This includes any cutting of the skin, surgeries, organ transplants, vaccines, shots, needles, injections, drug use, blood transfusions, tattoos, and piercings, anything that occurs where someone penetrates, pierces, or cuts the skin, causing blood to be released. This includes drinking blood, swearing an oath, becoming a blood brother, and it also includes the seemingly harmless practice of ear piercing. The above are just a few examples of blood covenants that bring a curse.

Father, in the name of Jesus, I repent for and renounce all blood covenants or oaths I have made. I ask You to forgive me for any act where I or someone has pierced, cut, or broken my skin that involves blood. I now break all soul-ties with all people whom I may have knowingly or unknowingly made a blood covenant or oath with. I send their souls and spirits back to them, and I call my soul and spirit back from them—cleansed and sanctified by the blood of Jesus Christ. Father, I now ask You to heal my mind and physical body and restore my soul.

I now command every unclean spirit that came into me through any and all blood covenants to *get out of me now* in the name of Jesus Christ. I now command every evil spirit that came into me through any and all blood covenants to *get out of me now* in the name of Jesus Christ. Father, I now ask You to heal my mind and physical body and restore my soul.

In Jesus' name,
Amen and amen!

22

PRAYER BEFORE AND AFTER SURGERY

Father, in the name of Jesus, I thank You for giving me power over all the power of the enemy. I exercise that power now—Satan, I bind you, rebuke you, and render you *powerless* over this (medical procedure, surgery, etc.). I bind the spirit of death that hovers over hospitals. I bind all bacterial and viral infections from entering my body. I bind excessive bleeding, complications, and medical mistakes. I employ mighty angels to go—now—to prepare the atmosphere in the operating room, recovery room, the hospital room I will be in, and assist the doctor, nurses, and all those who will have charge over me. I bind every evil soul-tie from forming due to medical staff, instruments, cutting, and all medical procedures. I cover myself with the blood of Jesus and commit my body to Your care until I am fully recovered. I speak a supernaturally quick recovery.

In Jesus' name,
Amen and amen!

23

PRAYER AGAINST BONDAGE

Note: This prayer deals primarily with forms of bondage that control your life; in other words, the vice that has a grip on you, including addiction.

Father, in the name of Jesus I repent and ask You to forgive me for running into a false refuge (an idol and idolatry) instead of running into You—the Prince of Peace, the Great Physician. The thing I ran to for false peace/comfort, etc. is ruling my life to the point where I have no peace at all. I want to be free from this bondage of [name of the vice]. I want to come out of this prison and be clean and free. I want the chains broken off of my life in this area. Forgive me if I judged others' weaknesses that caused the same thing to come to my house.

I break every evil soul-tie with [name of the vice].

I bind the strongman and break his power and command him to loose me and let me go in the name of Jesus.

I speak to every unclean spirit that came into me when I opened a door for the demons to come in, and I bind them and break their power and command them to *get out*! Come out of my bones, come out of my blood, come out of my mouth, my nose, my respiratory system, my organs, my bowels, and my stomach, come out of every area of my soul, body and my mind. I command you to *get out of me* in the name of Jesus Christ. I break your hold on me, I break the thoughts of it, I break the desire for it, and I break all cravings, in the name of Jesus. I bind the spirit of Pharmakia (see Mental Torment Prayer page 50), sorcery, and all witchcraft spirits. I break your power and command all spirits attached to the vice of _____ to get out of me now in the name of Jesus Christ.

Father, Your Word says, whosoever destroys this temple, him I will destroy (see 1 Cor. 3:17), therefore I ask You to forgive me for bringing destruction to my temple, and I now break the death sentence that I brought upon myself. I speak a reversal of damage as a result of my addiction and I speak healing to my body. (Please also see Healing Prayer page 31.) I apply the shed and resurrected blood of Jesus to my body and I apply *to myself—the grace that is sufficient* in order that I might be healed *and set free*. I thank You, Jesus, that You suffered on the cross so that I could be free and I thank You for it. I offer my body now as a living sacrifice and ask You to come live victoriously in me.

In Jesus' name I pray, and I give You thanks,
Amen and amen!

24

PRAYER AGAINST SATANIC ATTACK

Note: You can also pray this for someone else who is being attacked by inserting their name in place of yourself.

Father, I repent and ask You to forgive me for any door that was opened or that gave Satan and his demons license to attack me. I thank You that You forgive me. Your Word says that whosoever's sins are remitted, they are remitted—and right now I remit all sin in the name of Jesus Christ. Now I command every unclean spirit to leave me now in the mighty name of *Jesus*!

Father, right now, *in the name of Jesus*, I send mighty angels to be dispatched to me to stand shoulder to shoulder around me now so that I am totally hidden in Christ Jesus. I cover myself with the precious blood of Jesus and I bind the demonic strongman assigned to me. I break the power of the strongman and call on Your mighty angels to assist to spoil "his house"! I call on Michael the archangel and others to come and do warfare in the heavenlies over me for the battle that is going on for my soul.

Satan, I bind you, rebuke you, and render you powerless. I destroy every satanic seal on my life and command it to *be broken now, in Jesus' name!* I send the fire of God into the enemy's camp, I speak confusion to the enemy's camp! I speak deafness, dumbness, blindness, incapacitation, and paralysis to every tormenting demon assigned to me now in the name of Jesus Christ.

I break every spirit of backlash and retaliation intended for me from the kingdom of darkness, in the name of Jesus!

I send angels to remove the demonic veil, and I call down the veil of the bride of Christ. I take the sword of the Spirit and sever—*now*—every demonic tie to the kingdom of darkness! I speak destruction and loose the fire of God upon every demon and evil spirit and command them to *stay away* from me. I bind the destroyer, break his power, and command him to *go*! In the name of *Jesus*!

Father, I call on Your ministering angels to minister to me *afresh* today. I speak *peace* and restoration to my mind, emotions, body, soul, and spirit. I give you thanks.

In Jesus' name!

Amen and amen!

25

PRAYER CONCERNING SOUL-TIES AND RENUNCIATION OF SEXUAL SIN

A soul-tie is a powerful emotional bond or connection that ties or unites you with someone else. You can become bound to a person through your soul. A soul-tie in the Bible means knit, bound up, and clave or cleave. Cleave has a double meaning: to separate or to bring closer together.[9]

---

[9] Cleave (1692 Strong's)—a primitive root; to impinge, i.e., cling or adhere; figuratively to catch by pursuit; abide fast, cleave (fast together), to follow close (hard after), be joined (together); keep (fast). To cleave, to adhere, firmly, as if with glue; to be glued; hence to be attached to anyone, to be lovingly devoted. God desires that we be soul-tied to Him: "Thou shalt fear the Lord thy God; him shalt thou serve, and to him shalt thou cleave, and swear by his name." (Deut. 10:20; see also Deut. 11:22, 1 Sam. 25:29). Genesis Lexicon (p. 719) to bind up, to bind together; metaphor, "the life of my Lord shall be bound up in the bundle of the living God."

Demonic spirits can also take advantage of evil or ungodly soul-ties and use them to transfer spirits between one person and another. Ezekiel 23:17 says, "And the Babylonians came to her into the bed of love, and they defiled her with their whoredom, and she was polluted with them." Soul-ties are formed through close friendships, through vows, commitments and promises, and through physical intimacy.

Not all soul-ties are bad. God wants us to have healthy relationships that build us up, provide wisdom, and give godly counsel. God will strategically bring good relationships into our lives to form healthy soul-ties. "When David had finished speaking to Saul, the soul of Jonathan was knit with the soul of David, and Jonathan loved him as his own life" (1 Sam. 18:1). In contrast, Satan always brings counterfeits into our lives to form evil/ungodly soul-ties. Soul-ties can be formed by any type of immorality. A few ways evil soul-ties can be formed include abusive relationships (physically, sexually, emotionally, verbally), fornication, adulterous affairs, obsessive entanglements with a person (giving them more authority in your life than you give to God), and controlling relationships. Again remember that control is witchcraft.

Prayer: Father, in the name of the Lord Jesus Christ, I repent for all sin—including that of a sexual nature which came through my eyes, my ears, my mind, or through physical participation in sin. In particular, I confess the following:

all preoccupation with sexual and sensual desires and appetites and indulgences of them; all longing and ardent desire for what is forbidden (evil concupiscence); all inordinate affection, all unnatural and unrestrained passions and lusts; all promoting or partaking of that which tends to produce lewd emotions and foster sexual sin and lust.

I further confess all filthy communications: obscene and filthy language, conversation, and jokes; lewd and obscene music, poetry, literature, and art; all pornography; all acts of sodomy, adultery, immorality, fornication, oral sex, masturbation, effeminacy, and homosexuality. I also confess all perversions including affection for and attachment to philosophies, religions, and lifestyles that glorify, promote, and condone sexual conduct in thought, word, and deed, contrary to the standard for believers in the Bible.

Lord, I ask that You reveal other sexual offences in my life that I have committed. Father, I confess and renounce all unGodly involvement, both known and unknown, by me or my ancestors. I hate Satan, his demons and all his works; I count all that offends You, Father, as my enemy (see Ps. 139:21-24). I renounce all spirits of sexual sin. I declare all curses over my life, whether through my own sins or those of my ancestors, to be broken, particularly in the area of sexual sin and occult involvement. I claim freedom from all curses that have been placed upon me, in the name of Jesus Christ. I hereby reclaim all ground that I have ever given to Satan in body, mind, soul, or spirit. I dedicate it to you,

Lord, to be used for Your glory alone. I want You to control and empower every area of my life, including my body and temple; that from now on they might be used according to Your will. God, I now give to You my affections, emotions, and desires, and request that they might be motivated and controlled by Your Holy Spirit (see Rom. 12:1-2).

Father, in the name of Jesus I ask You to forgive me for hardening my heart against You when I sinned with _____. {Do this separately for every person you have fornicated with}. I send his/her soul and spirit back to her/him, and I call my soul and spirit back to me, cleansed and sanctified with the blood of Jesus Christ, and I ask You to restore my fragmented mind, my soul, my spirit, and my emotions in the name of Jesus.

I command every spirit that came into me through that sin to leave me now in the name of Jesus, and I give leave to every familiar spirit that attached itself to me. I command you to go now in Jesus' name.

I now reclaim the authority that I forfeited and I ask for Your Holy Spirit to come and fill the places that have been vacated, and I give you thanks.

In Jesus' name,
Amen and amen!

26

PRAYER CONCERNING FORGIVENESS

Unforgiveness brings darkness into your life. Unforgiveness and bitterness go hand and hand. Holding unforgiveness in our hearts leads to bitterness and this affects our relationship with God in a major way. We are to follow peace and holiness as a life practice and we cannot truly do that while harbouring unforgiveness. If we fail to forgive, bitterness will disconnect us from having a clear view of the Lord, thus in a sense cutting us off from God. Not only does it impact your relationship with God but it directly affects your relationship with yourself. You will begin to turn in on yourself and become self-critical, self-condemned, and rejected because of this evil root. Unforgiveness and bitterness result in many harmful and hurtful things. They tear the spirit; poison the soul; bring in deception; lead to immorality, build walls of isolation; and leave a trail of broken relationships. Satan gains legal right through your unforgiveness and can torment you in many ways.

Make a list of the people you need to forgive and also anyone you need to ask forgiveness from (both living and deceased). Ask the Holy Spirit to reveal anyone that you are resentful/harbouring bitterness towards, even unconsciously. You may not even realize that you are carrying around unforgiveness. Make sure you also include God on the list. Almost everyone without exception has blamed God for something. And lastly, forgive yourself. Say the following prayer separately for each person.

Lord, I confess that I have not loved, but have resented [name person] for their action(s) of [the action they did—examples: lied about me, gossiped, hurt me, rejected me, abused me, betrayed me, disappointed me, etc.] and as a result I have held unforgiveness, bitterness, resentment, and contempt towards [name them, both living and dead] in my heart. I repent for unforgiveness towards them and ask You to forgive me.

I now call upon You, Lord, to help me forgive them, and I do now as an act of my will choose to forgive [name person] and ask You to forgive them also, and bless them, Lord.

I do now forgive and accept myself. I give you thanks.
In Jesus' name,
Amen and amen!

27

PRAYER AGAINST GENERATIONAL CURSES

Blessings are desirable or beneficial things that God may grant. Curses are the opposite and bring punishment and painful conditions, experiences, and feelings. Before each of us God has set blessing or cursing, which must be chosen. (See Deuteronomy 11:26-28.)

Generational curses are curses and demonic afflictions that are passed down the bloodline, in other words are generationally inherited. If not broken in the name of Jesus, they can continue to transfer from one generation to the next, causing similar issues in the family.

Prayer: Father, I repent for the sins of my forefathers and renounce every evil they did all the way back to Adam and Eve. In the name of Jesus Christ, I break the generationally inherited curses that have come down upon me through my father's bloodline. Every unholy spirit that came to me from my father when I was conceived, I command you to get out of me now in Jesus' name, and I give leave to the familiar spirits that have followed me down my father's bloodline to track me, trace me, guard me, and guide me in ways that are contrary to God. Go, in the name of Jesus Christ. In the name of Jesus Christ, I break the generationally inherited curses that have come down upon me through my mother's bloodline. Every unholy spirit that came to me from my mother when I was conceived, I command you to get out of me now in Jesus' name, and I give leave to the familiar spirits that have followed me down my mother's bloodline to track me, trace me, guard me, and guide me in ways that are contrary to God. Go, in the name of Jesus Christ.

Say aloud, In the name of Jesus I bind, break and command out _____ (Name diseases, adverse personality traits, evil tendencies, etc.)

In the name of Jesus Christ, I now rebuke, break, and loose myself and my children from any and all evil curses, charms, vexes, hexes, spells, jinxes, psychic powers, bewitchments, witchcraft, sorcery, freemasonry, oaths, covenants, dedications, or ceremonies that were made on my behalf while I was in the loins of my forefathers.

I call down fire from God to destroy the altar that Satan has erected for my life, and I give leave to the unholy angel that Satan appointed to me at the time of my conception, in Jesus' holy name.

I thank You, Lord, for setting me free.

I now cover myself with the precious blood of Jesus Christ and give You thanks. I seal this deliverance.

In Jesus' name,
Amen and amen!

PRAYER AGAINST THE ANTICHRIST SPIRIT

One of the main workings of Satan's kingdom and his opposition to God and to the church of Jesus Christ is through the spirit of antichrist. The word *Christ* is from a Greek word *christos*, which exactly corresponds to the Hebrew word *Mashiach* from which we get Messiah. So when we say "antichrist," that means anti-Messiah. "Anti" is a Greek preposition. It has two meanings, first it means against, so the first operation is against Messiah. The second meaning is "in place of." The passage in 1 John 2:18-22 NKJV describes this:

> Children, it is the last hour; and as you have heard that the Antichrist is coming, even now many antichrists have come, by which we know that it is the last hour. They went out from us, but they were not of us; for if they had been of us, they would have continued with us; but they went out that they might be made manifest,

that none of them were of us. But you have an anointing from the Holy One, and you know all things. I have not written to you because you do not know the truth, but because you know it, and that no lie is of the truth. Who is a liar but he who denies that Jesus is the Christ?

The working of the spirit of antichrist is intensifying as we get closer to the end of the age and its ultimate purpose is to put a false Messiah in place of the true Messiah. The spirit of antichrist is extremely active almost throughout the whole professing church. In 1 John 4:2-3 we read:

By this you know the Spirit of God: Every spirit that confesses that Jesus [the Messiah] has come in the flesh is of God, and every spirit that does not confess that Jesus [the Messiah] has come in the flesh is not of God. And this is the spirit of the Antichrist, which you have heard was coming, and is now already in the world.

The spirit of antichrist is the spirit that operates through everything in opposition of Jesus Christ and John has given us certain marks of the spirit of antichrist that are very important. The antichrist spirit can be generationally inherited through the worship of other gods by our ancestors; being conceived out of wedlock; religions that do not embrace Jesus Christ as the Son of God come in the flesh and His death and resurrection, belief systems that are contrary to the Word of God; Christian religions that reject the Holy

Ghost, organizations requiring oaths, secret societies, and involvement with the occult, etc. are included.

Prayer: Father, I repent for all sins of my forefathers, including whoredoms, rebellion, idolatry and witchcraft that brought in the antichrist spirit and in the name of Jesus Christ, I bind and break the power of the generationally-inherited spirit of antichrist that came upon me through the religious doctrines of my forefathers. The doctrine that rejected the Holy Ghost and speaking in tongues; any doctrine that did not believe that Jesus was God in the flesh; the worship of other gods; any religion that does not accept the entire Word of God; the antichrist spirit working in Freemasonry, secret societies, or from participating in any form of the occult; from membership in any religion that Jesus Christ is not the center of; or however it came upon me. I pledge my allegiance to God the Father, God the Son Jesus Christ, and God the Holy Ghost, whom I will serve all the days of my life. Now I bind and break the power of the spirit of antichrist and command it to leave me now, in Jesus' name. I bind and break all associated spirits of antichrist and command them to leave me now, in Jesus name.

I now cover myself with the precious blood of Jesus Christ and give You thanks in Jesus' name. I seal this deliverance.

In Jesus' name,
Amen and amen!

29

PRAYER AGAINST THE SPIRIT OF DEATH, INCLUDING ABORTION

Note: If you have had an abortion (this includes the male partner involved and anyone who has encouraged or helped someone seek an abortion, driven someone to an abortion clinic, etc.), it is imperative you pray the abortion prayer below. This includes contemplating an abortion.

The spirit of death came upon all of us through Adam and Eve. God told Adam and Eve (see Gen. 2:17) not to eat from the tree of knowledge of good and evil, and that in the day they would eat of it they would surely die. We know they did not drop dead, but death entered into all mankind through the fall. The word *die* means a slow, gradual diminishing. When we get saved, the sin issue is dealt with, but death is not. After salvation, the power of the spirit of death needs to be broken and cast out. It is the ruler spirit over all infirmities. It's what causes us to age, decay, degenerate, and decrease in strength physically and mentally. This spirit hovers over hospitals, nursing homes, and highways. Some sins can bring a "death sentence" (see Lev. 20).

Abortion results in a strong curse that brings in the spirit of death. Our entire nation is under the curse of death through the legalization of abortion. The abortion spirit and curse of death goes undetected because it's usually a closely guarded secret. Again it is important to note that this is not just a woman who had an abortion, but the male involved in creating the pregnancy, and even the people who helped in that abortion in any form. It can even be from encouraging a woman to get an abortion, driving her to an abortion clinic, etc. This spirit of death from abortion can be the root of miscarriages, stillborn births, SIDS, infertility, problems in menstrual cycles, depression, suicide, cancers, insanity, (see Mental Torment, page 50) or fatal diseases. It can also result in the death of a marriage, relationships, finances, dreams, ministry, spiritual growth, and opportunities, etc.

"The Lord is long-suffering and abundant in mercy, forgiving iniquity and transgressions; but He by no means clears the guilty, visiting the iniquities of the fathers on the children to the third and fourth generations" (Num. 14:18 NKJV).

"The Lord is slow to anger and rich in unfailing love, forgiving every kind of sin and rebellion. Even so He does not leave sin unpunished, but punishes the children for the sins of their parents to the third and fourth generations" (Num. 14:18 NLT).

Father, in the name of Jesus Christ, I break the curse of death that came upon me through Adam and Eve. I bind and break the power of the spirit of death, the ruler spirit over all sickness and disease, and command it to get out of me now in the name of Jesus Christ.

I bind all degenerative diseases of the bones, eyes, blood, and organs. I come against the effects of aging: decay, physical weakness, mental weakness, infirmities of the aged, i.e., Alzheimer's, Dementia, Arthritis, impotence, senility, [name your infirmity], joint problems, heart disease, blood pressure problems, insomnia, constipation, loss of teeth, gums, muscle tone, etc., and I speak a reversal of damage right now to every working of death in my life up to this point. It is written in Romans 8:11, "If the same spirit that raised Christ from the dead dwells in me, it will quicken my mortal body." So I speak a quickening to my body right now, in Jesus' name. I speak resurrection life to every cell in my body. I speak a quickening to my muscles, joints, connective tissues, skin, organs, and blood, and I activate the mind of Christ that I received when I accepted You as my Savior.

I bind all fatal diseases: cancer, heart attacks, strokes, diabetes, [name yours and what runs in your bloodline]. I break its power off my life and command the spirit of death to leave me now, in the name of Jesus Christ.

I thank You, Father, that Your Son, Jesus Christ, abolished death (see 2 Tim. 1:10) and the law of death (see Rom. 8:2), so that I might live the abundant life You want me to have (see John 10:10).

I now cover myself with the precious blood of Jesus Christ and give You thanks in Jesus' name. I seal this deliverance.

In Jesus' name,
Amen and amen!

30

PRAYER CONCERNING ABORTION AND THE SHEDDING OF INNOCENT BLOOD

Father, in the name of Jesus, I ask You to forgive me for the sin of abortion. I ask You to forgive me for murder and the shedding of innocent blood. I break all ties with abortion. I break evil soul-ties with all those having any part in it: the male I conceived with, doctors, nurses, workers in clinics, advisors, parents, friends, even the person who helped me pay for it, drove me to the clinic, encouraged me to get an abortion, or assisted in any way. I send their souls and spirits back to them, and I call my soul and spirit back from them, cleansed and sanctified by the blood of Jesus Christ, and I ask You to restore my soul and heal my mind.

I thank You, Father, that in 1 John 1:9, You say that if I confess my sin, You are faithful and just to forgive my sin and to cleanse me from all unrighteousness. Thank You, Father, that I can be and am cleansed through the shed and resurrected blood of Your Son, Jesus Christ.

I now break the curse of death off my life. First, I break the curse of death that came upon me and all mankind through Adam and Eve's sin, which also caused all of mankind to be born separated from God and in need of a Savior. Second, I break the death sentence that came upon me through the participation in abortion and murder.

I now command out of me every spirit that came into me through the sin of abortion and murder. I bind and break the power of the spirits of death and murder and command them to get out of me now in Jesus' name. I bind and break the power of the unloving spirit, the hard heart, and command it to get out of me now, in the name of Jesus Christ. I speak to the voices in my head and command them to shut up and go. I bind and break the spirit of insanity, and I command every tormenting spirit to leave me now, in the name of Jesus Christ.

I now command out of me every spirit of self-destruction, spirits of anger and murderous rage, self-hatred, guilt, shame, suicidal thoughts of being unworthy to live, unworthy to be happy, all spirits of bondage, and all the things I have done to escape the pain. I command all the ways the spirit of death has been working in my life to be broken now and also broken off my children and grandchildren. Miscarriages, infertility, female problems, female cancers, multiple divorces, migraine headaches, nightmares, death (or abrupt ending) to relationships, dreams, plans, finances, happiness, etc. I now break the power of every evil spirit that's been working in my life as a result of abortion and command it to get out of my life once and for all. I am forgiven!

I now forgive myself. (Stop right here. Meditate on forgiving yourself. Truly receive the forgiveness of God and His goodness that He is pouring out upon you. Stop beating yourself up. Receive a fresh anointing of His love and be filled up with it.)

Lord, Jesus, I ask that You would go to my baby, and tell him/her how sorry I am. Ask him/her to please forgive me, and tell him/her that I look forward to seeing them when I get to heaven.

Now I command out of me all spirits of grief, sorrow, sadness, weeping, longing, heaviness, broken-heartedness, shame, guilt, and self-deprecation to get out of me! Go! In the mighty name of Jesus Christ of Nazareth. (Take a deep breath and let it out . . . however long it takes . . . let the healing work of the Holy Spirit be completed in you.)

I now cover myself with the precious blood of Jesus Christ and Father, I give You thanks in Jesus' name. I seal this deliverance.

In Jesus' name,
Amen and amen!

31

PRAYER AGAINST THE CURSE OF THE FIRSTBORN

This is a curse that typically comes onto the firstborn male in the family but can also go to the firstborn child, even a female. Exodus 13:2 says "Sanctify unto me all the firstborn, whatsoever openeth the womb among the children of Israel, both man and of beast: it is mine." So naturally, that's the one Satan wants the most! Luke 2:23 says, "As it is written in the law of the Lord, every male that openeth the womb shall be called holy to the Lord." Note—you can pray this over any first born by inserting their name in place of yours.

Prayer: Father, in the name of Jesus, I bind and break the power of the curse of the firstborn. Satan, I bind you, rebuke you, and render you powerless from my life! I call down fire from heaven to destroy the altar that you have erected for my life. I give leave to the unholy angel appointed to me at birth, I speak the blessings of God upon my life and I speak to the gifts that were given to me by God and cause those gifts to be activated to serve the living God all the days of my life. I bind my feet to the pathway of righteousness, in Jesus' name.

I now cover myself with the precious blood of Jesus Christ and give You thanks in Jesus' name. I seal this deliverance.

In Jesus' name,
Amen and amen!

PRAYER AGAINST THE SPIRIT OF THE BRIDE OF SATAN

There are some tactics that we as ministers have learned from former witches and Satanists. When we get saved we become the bride of Christ. Satan counterfeits God in all things so if Christians are the bride of Christ, then the people who belong to Satan effectually are the "bride of Satan." When a person has been involved in the occult, New Age or Satanism, etc, they are afflicted by this spirit. This spirit can be passed down through the bloodline (generationally inherited) from various forms of abuse (victimization) sexual abuse, physical abuse, emotional abuse, spiritual abuse, satanic abuse, gross sexual sin, molestation, prostitution, pornography, etc. Satan puts a spiritual veil on those and can "hide the person" in the spirit realm, causing a major block for a Christian to achieve what God wants to give him or her. Other spirits that come in with the spirit of the bride of Satan are Kundalini spirits, incubus spirits, succubus spirits (see Incubus and Succubus page 108), masturbation, whoredom, fornication, spirits of the "old maid"/"lifelong bachelor," lust, seducing spirits, rape, incest, pedophilia, and molestation.

Prayer: Father, in the name of Jesus, I bind and break the power of the spirit of the bride of Satan. I break every oath, covenant, and dedication that was made on my behalf when I was in the loins of my forefathers.

Satan, right now I give you a spiritual writ of divorcement. *I am not your bride!* You will have no further access to my body. I am the bride of Christ. Right now I remove from myself your veil, Satan! (You may even want to go through the motion of pulling his veil off your head.) This veil has caused me to be hidden from the things of God and has even stopped me from knowing/meeting/identifying my future husband/wife.

I give leave to the familiar spirits that operate with the spirit of the bride of Satan, Kundalini spirits, incubus spirits, succubus spirits, masturbation, whoredom, fornication, spirits of "the old maid," "lifelong bachelor," lust, seducing spirits, rape, incest, pedophilia, and molestation.

I break evil soul-ties with [name of offender], who touched me in an unholy manner. I send their souls and spirits back to them, and I call my soul and spirit back to myself—cleansed and sanctified by the blood of Jesus Christ—and I give leave to the familiar spirits that attached themselves to me.

I now command every unclean spirit that came into me by them to *go* in the name of Jesus Christ.

I now reclaim all authority that was forfeited over myself, and I thank You, Father, for making me whole again.

Father, I now ask You to drop down from heaven the veil of the bride of Christ, to whom I am wed, for I am the bride of Christ.

I now cover myself with the precious blood of Jesus Christ and give You thanks in Jesus' name. I seal this deliverance.

In Jesus' name,
Amen and amen!

33

PRAYER AGAINST THE CURSE OF THE BASTARD

This is a very powerful curse that plagues almost every believer with few exceptions. "A person begotten out of wedlock shall not enter into the assembly of the Lord; even until his tenth generation shall his descendants not enter into the congregation of the Lord" (Deut. 23:2). Ten generations is a period of four hundred years. The grace of the Lord Jesus Christ, who bore this curse when He hung on the tree, gives us a way out. Galatians 3:13 reads, "Christ hath redeemed us from the curse of the law, being made a curse for us; for it is written, Cursed is every one that hangeth on a tree." This is not automatic. You must appropriate this Scripture to your life.

The curse of the bastard is often associated with illegitimacy but it's important to remember: You don't get this curse *only* if your parents had you out of wedlock. There are many other reasons this curse comes in and it is generationally inherited. People with this curse often have a profound feeling of rejection, causing them to withdraw or be attention seekers. There is either timidity, (fear) or rage (suppressed anger), with no real in between. Those who are not properly disciplined, loved, or nurtured often fail to achieve spiritual intimacy. The curse often manifests in being unable to receive God's love (see Heb. 12:5-8; Rom. 5:1-4; 1 John 4:18). They are unable to enter into the deeper things of God.

Generally, there is an unloving spirit with the curse of the bastard and so a feeling of rejection and abandonment is often felt. This can make you feel like God hates you or is mad at you. You feel like no one really loves you and this produces an inability to love or receive love, despite being assured by various loved ones (which results in an inability to lead your children into a godly life, etc.).

Other manifestations may include feeling like a black sheep; you don't fit in, inability to feel welcome or at peace in God's house. Other symptoms can include rebellion, delinquency, sickness, suicide, depression, murder, and mental illness (see mental torment prayer, pg. 50). Other symptoms are never feeling at home anywhere for long (even a church), never really being able to make connections with people; often having strained relationships, feeling dissatisfied and discontent in many areas of life, never really feeling good about yourself. Often these people have all types of fears. This person can become a workaholic, striving excessively to succeed, or be works oriented or have a fear of failure, fear of or resisting authority, fighting verbally and physically, being predisposed to sexual activities, not experiencing much joy in natural or spiritual life. These are just a few examples of the bastard curse.

Prayer: Father God, I bring before you today every sin of my forefathers all the way back to Adam and Eve. I ask You to forgive the sin of illegitimacy that is in my family line all the way back to Adam and Eve. I ask You to forgive all the sin that has displeased You, or if there has been anyone who has hated You and is bearing this iniquity, I ask You to forgive them also. Lord, Your Word says that we bear the sins and the iniquities of our forefathers, and I ask You to cleanse my bloodline now of anything that I have inherited from my forefathers.

Father, in the name of Jesus, I bind and break the power of the curse of the bastard and I command it to go now in Jesus' name. I command out every unclean[10] and familiar spirit[11] that came into me through this curse and all attached demons to *go now* in the name of Jesus Christ. I bind and break the unloving spirit that came in and command it to go in Jesus' name. I now call out all associated spirits and when I say your name you have to leave in Jesus' name. All spirits of rejection, rejection by others, rejection of others, rejec-

---

[10] See Unclean Spirit in Glossary page 126
[11] See Familiar Spirits in Glossary page 125

tion by God, rejection by father, rejection by mother, self-rejection, self-hatred, suicide, wishing you could die, wishing you were never born, oppression, depression, repression, blaming God, needy spirit, needing constant reassurance, never satisfied, insecurity, discontentment, loneliness, loner, the black sheep, alienation, not fitting in, lawlessness, and rebellion: I command you to go in Jesus' name. All fear spirits, all phobias, go now in Jesus' name.

Inferiority complex, poor image, low self-esteem, unworthy, not good enough, perfectionism, works oriented, workaholic, being driven all the time, overachiever—all those spirits go now in Jesus' name!

Unloving spirit, unable to give or receive love or experience the love of God, not being interested in the things of God, being unable to receive or enter into the things of God.

Hurt, betrayal, abandonment, rejection, jealousy, envy, resentment, rage, anger, fighting, spirit of the ravager, go now in Jesus' name. All spirits of bondage, bondage to drugs, alcohol, tobacco, gluttony, eating disorders, all addictions, pornography, obsessive-compulsive behaviours, inordinate affection for anything. Escapism, shopping, gambling, video games, all addictions *go now in Jesus' name*.

I speak restoration of all the damage this curse has caused. I speak healing to my mind, will, and emotions in Jesus' name.

I loose the spirit of adoption whereby I cry Abba Father—adoption as a child of God.

I now cover myself with the precious blood of Jesus Christ and give You thanks in Jesus' name. I seal this deliverance.

In Jesus' name,
Amen and amen!

34

PRAYER AGAINST THE CURSE OF TAMAR

Second Samuel 13:1 begins the story of Absalom, Tamar, and Amnon. Tamar was raped by her brother Amnon, and then her other brother, Absalom, tells her to keep quiet about it. So many times things happen in families that are swept under the rug. When they're not dealt with, they grow. Tamar was shamed, thus she thought herself to be inferior, dirty, etc. This is what desolation does, and the enemy works through desolation to cause other manifestations.

The devil has the most power in the area of secrecy. Arrested development is a frequent manifestation of desolation. This curse of Tamar can come in through rape, molestation, incest, or any kind of sexual abuse. It is important that you forgive the offender/violator (see Forgiveness Prayer page 76). If you were abused in any way, you have to know it was not your fault and what happened to you was not in any way okay. Because "we wrestle not with flesh and blood," the real offender was Satan using the offender/violator person to do his dirty deed.

Prayer: Father, in the name of Jesus, I bind and break the power of the curse of Tamar and I command out every unclean and familiar spirit that came into me through this curse of Tamar and all attached demons to *go now* in the name of Jesus Christ. I bind, break, and command all the following to go now in Jesus' name: spirits of rape, molestation, incest, sexual abuse, cruelty, inappropriate touch, lustful looks, forced oral sex, forced anal sex, perversion, physical pain, emotional pain, mental pain, all fear, Magor Missabib "terror on every side" (see Jer. 20:3) fright, shock, trauma. All fears including; fear of the dark, fear of certain places (like wherever it happened), fear of strangers, fear of trusting anyone, fear of sex, frigidity/impotence, fear of becoming pregnant, fear of death, fear of violence, fear of being killed, fear of men, fear of the offender, fear of those in authority, fear of it happening again, fear of being found out, fear of going to sleep, etc. I command you to go in Jesus' name.

I bind and break the power of nightmares, insomnia, memory recall, nervousness, anger/rage/retaliation, bitterness, resentment, betrayal, unforgiveness, hatred, self-hatred, all self-destructive behaviours, all bondages, drugs, alcohol, food, sex, shopping, gambling, cutting, escaping or anesthetizing the pain, idolatry, fantasy, promiscuity, provocative dress, seductive behaviour, whoredom or whoremongering, fornication, masturbation, etc. Go now in Jesus' name!

I bind and break the power of the "mean man," monster, torturer, rapist, violator, the one who inflicts pain, the pervert, abuser, incubus/succubus, lust, tormentors, tormenting thoughts, unclean spirits, spirits of the ravager, triggers: sights, sounds, smells, textures. Go now in Jesus' name.

I command all grief, sorrow, sadness, oppression, depression, death wishes, suicidal thoughts, loneliness, seclusion, stupor, foggy-mindedness, dismay, insanity, confusion, hopelessness, numbness, to *go* in the name of Jesus Christ. I command every spirit that came into me through that sin to leave me now in the name of Jesus, and I give leave to every familiar spirit that attached itself to me—I command you to go now in Jesus' name.

I break off me and my descendants all desolation that came upon me generationally or through rape, molestation, incest or physical, mental, or emotional abuse.

I now break the evil soul-ties with [name of the offender].

I send [name of offender]'s soul and spirit back to him/her, and I call my soul and spirit back to me, cleansed and sanctified with the blood of Jesus Christ, and Father I ask You to restore my fragmented mind, my soul, my spirit, and my emotions in the name of Jesus.

I command every spirit that came into me through the curse of Tamar to leave me now in the name of Jesus, and I give leave to every familiar spirit of the curse of Tamar that attached itself to me—I command you to go now in Jesus' name.

Father, I ask that You restore to me the purity that was stolen from me. I now reclaim the authority that I forfeited and I ask for Your Holy Spirit to come and fill the places that have been vacated, in Jesus' name.

I now cover myself with the precious blood of Jesus Christ and give You thanks in Jesus' name. I seal this deliverance.

In Jesus' name,
Amen and amen!

35

PRAYER AGAINST THE CURSE OF JEZEBEL AND AHAB

The relationship of Ahab and Jezebel provides an excellent illustration of the curse brought about by a husband and wife being out of God's divine order for a family. This curse goes all the way back to Adam and Eve. In the Bible, Queen Jezebel is presented as a prime example of female dominance and witchcraft (see 1 Kings 16:22; 2 Kings 9). In Revelation 2:18-29, the false prophetess of Thyatira is labeled as Jezebel.

Jezebel women are characterized by their attempts to control those around them through false teachings and the use of occult power. Jezebel can also parade her schemes under the cover of religion and "good" motives. With her wiles and witchcraft, Queen Jezebel persuaded her husband to allow her to usurp authority in the kingdom. Christian men and women today are often deceived and driven by the religious pretensions of these demonic forces. The Jezebel influence is rooted in witchcraft, sorcery, and idolatry and causes women to forsake the protection and place given to them in God's Word.

There is also a corresponding or complementary spirit to Jezebel, which we call the Ahab spirit. This brings destruction of the family priesthood, laziness, and sluggishness in males who allow females to dominate and control but despise and hate them for it. The spirit of Jezebel enters the family situation wherever God's order of authority is either not known or ignored.

God's order is basically simple: The authority of man is Christ; the authority of woman is man; the authority of Christ is God (see 1 Corinthians 11:3). Nothing can change the fact that the head of every woman is man. Any tampering with God's structuring of family authority will open the man, women and children to curses and satanic attack.

The Ahab spirit, rooted in the destruction of the family priesthood, causes a man to forsake his responsibilities as the head of the household. Ahab men are weak spiritually and are often wrongly influenced by women, particularly their wives. The Ahab man lets the woman "wear the pants." He will not only refuse to take the spiritual headship, but often will not take responsibility for working to make the living for the wife and children. He has overlooked the Scriptural admonition that a man who does not work should not eat (see 2 Thess. 3:10), and that if a man fails to provide for his own, he has denied the faith and is worse than an infidel (see 1 Tim. 5:8).

A man is to provide both spiritual and material security for his family. If he cannot or will not, he is in trouble with God. When you have a Jezebel or Ahab spirit, you will not commit to God, family, children, home. This spirit also shifts the blame to the other spouse. The man's role is as the spiritual umbrella of protection for his wife and children; he is charged with the role of prophet and priest for them.

Prayer: Father, I confess and renounce as sin, and repent for everything I have ever done to manipulate, dominate, and control other people, or allowed these actions as Ahab did. I bind, break and command out the foul Jezebellic spirits and Ahab spirits in the name of Jesus. I declare every curse having to do with Jezebel and Ahab and associated spirits, spirits from whatever source, all the way back to Adam and Eve, on both sides of my family, to be broken in Jesus' name.

I sever any ties of bondage that may exist between me and those who have practiced sorcery, witchcraft, and mind control against me. I bind, break, and command out all spirits causing rebellion and idolatry against proper authority in the home and in the church; and all curses of matriarchal control. I bind and break the power of all spirits of rejection, witchcraft control, and idolatry and command you to go now in Jesus' name. I command all familiar spirits that came in through Jezebel and Ahab to *go now* in the name of Jesus Christ of Nazareth. And now, Father, I surrender my mind, will, and emotions to You in accordance with Your Word on how a godly man/woman is to conduct themselves. Heal my mind, will, and emotions in Jesus' name. Help me to come into true submission to You, Father, in Jesus' name.

I now cover myself with the precious blood of Jesus Christ and give You thanks in Jesus' name. I seal this deliverance.

In Jesus' name,
Amen and amen!

36

PRAYER AGAINST SPIRITS OF INCUBUS AND SUCCUBUS

These are demonic spirits that typically sexually attack males and females. These spirits operate through witchcraft spells, sexual sin, perversion, and curses of lust, idolatry, harlotry, and whoredom and can be generationally inherited curses. Chemosh[12] (see 1 Kings 11:7, 33) was the demon god worshipped by the Moabites and Ammonites, an incestuous generational line of Lot and his daughters. Incubus/Succubus are filthy spirits that sexually attack the victim while asleep, and may force intercourse. This also may occur through sodomy, oral sex, or anal sex. Typically, these demonic spirits cause lustful dreams and even sleep paralysis, followed by tormenting the individual

---

[12] Chemosh was the deity of the Moabites and Amonites whose name most likely meant "destroyer" or "subduer." This is the incestuous linage of Lot having intercourse with his daughters.

with guilt and condemnation. The victim often reports feeling paralyzed and in some cases cannot speak. The attack is not always for sexual reasons, but may be to cause bodily harm as well. It is typically thought that Succubus is a female demon that attacks a human male, and Incubus is a male demon that attacks a human female, but that is unlikely, as demons are disembodied spirits that have no gender but can take on the form of a male or female.

Incubus: demon(s), in the form of a male, operating through sexual intercourse with a sleeping woman

Succubus: demon(s), in the form of a female, operating through sexual intercourse with a sleeping man

Prayer: Father, I repent and renounce every sin, including sexual sin or any behaviour that caused these Incubus and Succubus demons to operate in my life. I repent and renounce all generationally inherited curses of lust, idolatry, incest, harlotry, and whoredom and I repent for all behavior, either my own or indirectly down my family line all the way back to Adam and Eve.

In the name of Jesus Christ, I bind the spirits of Incubus/Succubus, spirit wives, spirit husbands, I break your power and command you to get out of me now in the name of Jesus Christ. All sex spirits, anal sex, oral sex, bestiality, all spirits of perversion, I command you to get out of me now in Jesus' name. I bind and break sleep disorders, sleep apnea, sleep paralysis, night terrors, nightmares, and narcolepsy, and I command you to get out in Jesus' name.

Spirits causing barrenness, fertility issues, stillborn, miscarriage, I command you to get out now. Spirits of seduction and defilement, I command you to come out of me now in Jesus' name. Spirits of Kundalini, witchcraft, sorcery, incantations, greed, envy, perversion, incest, lust, whoredom, idolatry, and all spirits attached to Incubus and Succubus, get out of me now in the name of Jesus Christ. I bind and break the power of the spirit of Chemosh and command it to go in Jesus' name. I bind all the spirits of the Moabites and Ammonites (incest) and all associated spirits to get out of me now in the name of Jesus Christ. I loose off myself judgments and punishments from iniquity, idolatry, perversion, defilement, and whoredoms and command you to come out of me now in Jesus' name.

Father, I ask You to restore all fragmented areas, damaged areas, including the pineal gland and all hormonal dysfunction and any areas of my body that were damaged. I loose restoration and healing now to my body and I reclaim the authority that I forfeited and I ask for Your Holy Spirit to come and fill the places that have been vacated, in Jesus' name.

I now cover myself with the precious blood of Jesus Christ and give You thanks in Jesus' name. I seal this deliverance.

In Jesus' name,
Amen and amen!

37

PRAYER AGAINST THE SPIRIT OF LEVIATHAN

There is a strong evil spirit named Leviathan that we have repeatedly encountered. Pride and Leviathan are practically synonymous. Oftentimes there is an Egyptian spirit tied in with Leviathan, a spirit of the world and worldliness. Leviathan is associated with water and the ocean and is pictured with multiple heads. (See Ps. 74:13-14.) He is king over all the children of pride. (See Job 41:1-34.) By his spirit he has garnished the heavens; his hand has formed the crooked serpent. (See Job 26:13.) Leviathan particularly hates the first and second commandments. (See Ps. 104:26.) In that day the Lord with His great and strong sword shall punish Leviathan the piercing serpent, even Leviathan that crooked serpent; and He shall slay the dragon that [is] in the sea. (See Isa. 27:1, 26:5.)

Prayer: In the name of Jesus, I bind every spirit of Leviathan and all familiar spirits with Leviathan. I bind and break all pride, including the spirit of pride; the foot of pride (see Ps. 26:11); rod of pride (see Prov. 14:3); crown of pride (see Isa. 28:1, 3); great pride (see Jer. 13:9); pride of life (see 1 John 2:16).

I bind the haughty spirit (see Isa. 2:16), head held high, flirting eyes, walking with mincing, seductive steps, bejewelled foot of pride, transgression, no fear of God, flattery, vanity, iniquity, deceit, lack of wisdom, evil, mischief, narcissism, selfishness, the stiff-necked rebel, stubbornness, masculine and feminine superiority, the orator, rebellion, false ministry, and the false minister. I bind contempt, loftiness, all spirits exalting themselves above God, snares, contention, and foolishness. In Jesus' name I bind you, break your power, and command you to go.

I loose the spirit of humility and meekness and the mind of Christ, and I loose Godly strength, counsel, excellence, knowledge, wisdom, understanding, rest, and refreshing in Jesus' name.

I cover myself with the precious blood of Jesus Christ and give You thanks in Jesus' name. I seal this deliverance in the name of Jesus.

In Jesus' name,
Amen and amen!

38

PRAYER AGAINST THE SPIRIT OF KUNDALINI

Awakening the Kundalini is the expression used by mystics, Hindu gurus, and New Agers for the practice of focusing on a "serpent spirit" energy in the form of a coiled snake located at the base of the spine. Through meditation and physical body positioning, the aim is to "raise the Kundalini" through spiritual waypoints—called Chakras—located along the spine. The goal is to elevate the Kundalini spirit to the "Crown Chakra," which is located at the top of the head and is the source or originator of the presence of the third eye, which the kingdom of darkness depicts in the center of the forehead that opens one to receiving demonic vision, etc. These practices are often linked with yoga, eastern meditation, and mysticism. Yoga positions, chanting, visualization, and self-hypnotic routines can be one way to receive this demonic Kundalini spirit. Also people that are involved in any form of martial arts can receive this spirit as well.

It is worth noting that Kundalini spirit has been entering Christian churches across the world, even in North America. It causes people to have manifestations that they think is the Holy Spirit. They feel electric, or feel like they are on fire, or they make strange animal noises, i.e., hissing like snakes, barking like dogs, jerking around, making weird violent movements, jerking movements, thrashing around, convulsing, crawling around the floor, making weird noises, and it can result in people claiming visions, dreams, and feelings of peace and euphoria. This can include types of laughter. Again, it tries to mimic the Holy Ghost, but only the most discerning are seeing it for what it is. If you have been involved in any yoga, eastern meditation, mysticism, New Age or martial arts, you may have brought in the Kundalini spirit and associated spirits and it is imperative that you repent, renounce it, and cast these spirits out in the name of Jesus.

Prayer: Father God, I repent for opening any door that may have caused the Kundalini and associated spirits to come in. I now renounce all association with Satan, through witchcraft, sorcery, divination, and necromancy, all spirits working through Eastern mysticism, reincarnation, transcendental meditation, soul travel, martial arts, all wicked spirits working through mantras, tantra, yantra, chakras, all spirits of yoga, ying and yang, visualization, spirit guides, ascended masters, crystals, universal intelligence, and all related spirits. Say, "Satan, I renounce you and all your demons and I am closing every door to you that I have ever opened."

Father, in the name of the Lord Jesus Christ, I bind the strongman and every stronghold of Satan and his demons. I bind and break the power of the Kundalini spirit and all associated spirits, and I give you leave in Jesus' name. I now call on the mighty angels to come by the legions to attack, bind, and pull down the works of all these spirits, including mind control and mind-binding spirits. I bind, rebuke, and cast out all evil spirits of witchcraft, occult, New Age, sorcery, divination, necromancy, all spirits of Eastern mysticism, ascended masters, spirit guides, reincarnation, transcendental meditation, soul travel, martial arts, all wicked spirits working through mantra, tantra, yantra, chakras, all spirits of yoga, yin and yang, visualization, crystals, or universal intelligence. I command you to go in Jesus' name.

Now one by one go through the following list. Call out the name of each individual pose (the pose terms are not in the original Sanskrit name, but rather the pose name in Western culture).

Say aloud, "I command all spirits that came in through each pose to get out in the name of Jesus! Name the following poses:

"Bharadvaja's twist, big toe pose, boat pose, bound angle pose, bow pose, bridge pose, camel pose, cat pose, chair pose, child's pose, cobra pose, corpse pose, cow pose, crane pose, crow pose, dolphin plank pose, dolphin pose, downward-facing dog pose, eagle pose, easy pose, extended hand-to-big-toe pose, extended puppy pose, extended side angle pose, extended triangle pose, peacock pose, fire log pose, firefly pose, fish pose, four-limbed staff pose, garland pose, gate pose, half frog pose, frog pose, half lord of the fishes pose, half moon pose, headstand pose, handstand pose, head-to-knee forward bend, hero pose, heron pose, high lunge, low lunge, lion pose, crescent pose, crescent variation, all side poses, side stretch pose, all twist poses, legs-up-the-wall pose, locust pose, lotus pose, lord of the dance pose, mariachi pose, monkey pose, mountain pose, noose pose, all one-legged poses, all plank poses, plow pose, all reclining poses, scale pose, all bend poses, all side poses, staff pose, standing forward bend, standing half forward bend, standing split, supported headstand, supported shoulder stand, tree pose, triangle pose, upward bow (wheel) pose, upward facing two-foot staff pose, upward plank pose, upward salute, upward-facing dog pose, warrior I pose, warrior II pose, warrior III pose, wide-angle seated forward bend, wide-legged forward bend, all meditations, and all breath retentions. I bind, break, and command every spirit that I just named and even the ones I don't know the names of, to come out of me now in Jesus' name.

I now cover myself with the precious blood of Jesus Christ and give You thanks in Jesus' name. I seal this deliverance.

In Jesus' name,
Amen and amen!

39

BINDING AND LOOSING

Binding and loosing spirits is one of the most neglected powers that we have that God has given us. It is not complicated. We see from Matthew 16:19 and Matthew 18:18 that we are given the keys of the kingdom to bind and loose. A simple prayer will do: "I take authority over the spirits of [name the behavior, i.e., anger] in the person, [you, your spouse or your child], I bind you in the name of Jesus Christ.

When you bind a spirit in yourself or in others, that spirit is not able to manifest. The reason we bind is to cause the spirit not to operate in any way.

To loose spirits (angels) of God, say, "Father, I ask You in the name of Jesus Christ to send spirits of [name the ones desired] to hinder and stop the work of the enemy in [name of person]."

Example: If your mate has a spirit of anger, you can bind that spirit of anger. Do not do this to their face, rather go to another area, and you can not only bind the spirit but you can command it to get out in Jesus' name. You can then loose the spirit of "peace" in the situation or the opposite of whatever you are binding. Another interesting variation of binding and loosing which has proved effective is to bind evil and negative thoughts in yourself and other people. Specific edifying and positive spirits can be released at the same time (Matthew 18:18).

40

DO I HAVE TO KNOW THE NAME OF A SPIRIT TO BIND IT OR CAST IT OUT?

If you are unsure of a demon, names can be used to identify it. You receive a name at birth that identifies you for life. Demons also have names that identify them but more than that, those names identify the work that they do to destroy lives. The devil and his demons do not want you to know that they are at work in and over your life or the lives of your loved ones. They do not want to be exposed. They operate best in a person's life in obscurity and darkness. When light comes in they are exposed and through binding them and casting them out in Jesus' name, their power is broken and their work is destroyed. If identification of the demon by name is not known, then calling it out by description of its behavior is the next best step. Identifying spirits by what they do, their characteristics and by what they produce has the same effect on them. They now know that you have identified them and are speaking to them.

Here is an example of not knowing the name of an evil spirit, but knowing the effects of what it does. Call it out in this descriptive way, "You, the one that travels in the blood," or "You, the one that attacks the liver," or "You, the one that causes arguments," or "You, the one that is always making me lose my job," or "You, the one that is always making me lose my temper." Personify the demon by saying, "*You, the one that* . . . and then fill in the blank by describing what it does, causes or produces in your life.

Say the following aloud: "You, the one that [describe what it does], I bind you, break your power, and command you to go now in the name of Jesus Christ."

WHAT MUST I DO TO BE SAVED?

The prayers and deliverance contained in this book will be ineffective for a non-believer. In order for these prayers to work you must be a born-again believer in the Lord Jesus Christ. First of all, it is important to realize that there is only one way to God, and that is salvation through Jesus Christ, the Lord and Savior of the world (see John 14:6). The Word of God says if you believe with your heart that God raised Jesus from the dead, and confess Jesus as your Lord, you will be saved (see Rom. 10:9-10).

Salvation is a free gift that God offers us because of His unconditional love through the sacrifice Jesus made on our behalf: "But God commendeth his love toward us, in that, while we were yet sinners, Christ died for us" (Rom 5:8). That should remove any doubts about being worthy to be saved. Salvation is not something we deserve, nor is it something we can earn. It is a gift that was purchased and paid for by the blood of Jesus. Through the cross, God laid the punishment for our sin on Jesus so that we might have right standing with God through faith in Him (see 2 Cor. 5:21).

"For God so loved the world that He gave His only begotten Son, that whoever believes in Him should not perish but have everlasting life" (John 3:16). Right now, you can make a decision to accept and receive Jesus as your Saviour and proclaim Him Lord of your life. Pray the following prayer out loud and mean it with all of your heart:

"Heavenly Father, I come to You in the name of Jesus. Your Word says, 'Everyone who calls on the name of the Lord will be saved' (Acts 2:21). I am calling on You. I pray and ask Jesus to come into my heart and be Lord over my life according to Romans 10:9-10: 'That if thou shalt confess with thy mouth the Lord Jesus, and shalt believe in thine heart that God hath raised him from the dead, thou shalt be saved. For with the heart man believeth unto righteousness; and with the mouth confession is made unto salvation.'

"I believe that Jesus Christ died for me on the cross of Calvary, that He was buried and resurrected from the dead on the third day and ascended up into glory. I believe He will come again to judge the living and the dead. I now confess all my sins and repent. I ask You to forgive me and cleanse me from all sin. I now surrender my life to you Jesus and make You my Lord and Saviour. Thank You for redeeming me, cleansing me, justifying me, and sanctifying me in Your blood. I now give You permission to rule and reign in my heart from this day forward. Come into my life and fill me with Your Spirit, in Jesus' name, amen."

If you have repented of your sins and received Jesus Christ into your heart, you are now reborn! This is because the blood of Jesus Christ at the cross has washed you and cleansed you from all your sin and taken that burden off of you. You are now a Christian—a child of Almighty God! We want to welcome you into the family of God!

You now must be baptized in water and be filled with His Holy Spirit. We read in Acts 2:37-39:

> Now when they heard this, they were pricked in their heart, and said unto Peter and to the rest of the apostles, Men and brethren, what shall we do? Then Peter said unto them, Repent, and be baptized every one of you in the name of Jesus Christ for the remission of sins, and ye shall receive the gift of the Holy Ghost. For the promise is unto you, and to your children, and to all that are afar off, even as many as the Lord our God shall call.

Congratulations! **We would like to help you take the next steps in becoming a disciple of Jesus. Please contact the authors (info on the last page).**

GLOSSARY OF TERMS

Binding and Loosing – See page 118 for full description.

Bind the Strongman – After Jesus had cast out a devil and healed a deaf and mute boy, Jesus explained that in order to overturn the works and activity of the devil, we must bind him first. "Or else how can one enter a strong man's house and plunder his goods, unless he first binds the strong man? And then he will plunder his house" (Matt. 12:29). In order to neutralize the devil's works, we must go and deal directly with the source and bind up the devil so that his hands are tied. Then we'll be able to take back what he's stolen and bring a halt to his actions.

Familiar Spirits – The word *familiar* is from the Latin *familiaris*, meaning a "household servant," and is intended to express the idea that sorcerers had spirits as their servants ready to obey their commands. A "familiar spirit" is the designation of a specific type of evil spirit. It is so classified because of its chief characteristic: namely, familiarity. It is a relationship, a familiarity, with a person or personality and travels down the generational bloodline. (See Lev. 19:31, 20:27, 1 Sam. 28:7-9, 1 Chron. 10:13, 2 Chron. 33:6, Isa. 29:3-4, 2 Cor. 11:4, 13-15.)

Spirit of the Mean Man – An unusually cruel and hateful spirit in a person marked by a callous coldness and "mean-spirited" nature.

Unclean Spirits – Spirits of defilement, unclean and immoral in nature and activities that travel with every grouping of spirits. (See Mark 1:23, Mark 1:32-34, Mark 5:1-20, Luke 8:26-39, Matt. 8:28-34; Rev. 16:13-16.)

CONTACT US

Carla Butaud
carlabutaud@gmail.com

Sheila Zilinsky
sheilazilinsky@hotmail.com

AFTERWORD

We know we're not going to cover every prayer for every situation in life but now that you have started using these prayers you can start formulating & tailoring your own prayers from our examples. Get creative using Gods Word!

Start journaling and record the amazing things God is going to do in and through you!

We look forward to hearing your testimony!

Made in the USA
Monee, IL
12 July 2022